the essential guide to
Buying and Selling
Unquoted Businesses

the
essential guide
to
Buying and Selling Unquoted Businesses

Ian Smith

THOROGOOD
THE PUBLISHING BUSINESS
OF THE HAWKSMERE GROUP

Published by
Thorogood Ltd
12-18 Grosvenor Gardens
London SW1W 0DH
0171-824 8257

A catalogue record for this book is available from
the British Library.

September 1997

ISBN 1-85418-007-X

Printed in Great Britain by Ashford Colour Press.

Acknowledgements

I would like to thank various people who assisted in the production of this book namely Kevin Jewell, head of research at Capita Corporate Finance, Michele Crosier for typing the many drafts of the original manuscript and producing a readable first draft for submission to the publishers. The proof-reading of the book by my fellow deal leaders at Capita ensured that all obvious errors were spotted early in the process (hopefully)! In addition I am grateful for contributions and observations by fellow professionals and friends.

Ian Smith

June 1997

The author

Ian Smith, BA, CA

Ian Smith is Managing Director of Capita Corporate Finance Limited.

Capita Corporate Finance Limited has established a reputation for innovative financial advice to its clients in both the public and private sectors.

It is a wholly owned subsidiary of The Capita Group Plc, which itself was a buy-out from CIPFA in 1987 and subsequently obtained a Stock Market listing in 1989.

Ian specialises in acquisition and divestment work and has completed dozens of deals over the past ten years for a range of private and public sector clients.

At 38 he still expects to be leading deals for clients for many years to come.

Prior to joining Capita he held several senior positions within the Thomson Corporation, developed a leading UK Corporate Finance Boutique and enjoyed a brief spell with Mercury Asset Management.

Ian regularly presents seminars for independent companies on acquisitions, disposals and management buy-outs. His passion for athletics reached its height in 1987 when he joined the Scottish athletics squad at 800m and was a member of the winning Haringey British League team. These days his spare time is spent at his home in Hertfordshire with his wife and two young daughters.

CONTENTS

APPENDICES

Introduction

The buying and selling of unquoted businesses is a complex affair which lends itself to a rigorous route map to ensure success.

From a distance it may seem that buying is the opposite of selling. This is not the case. The executive who has completed numerous acquisitions does not necessarily possess the skills to execute a disposal at an attractive price.

This book separates the two processes of buying and selling. In reading the section on acquisitions the reader is taken through the chronological series of steps which should ensure well priced and structured deals. These steps are explored in detail within a framework called **The Acquisition Approvals Model.**

The model covers all aspects of the acquisition process from the first important stage of strategic direction through to a comprehensive review of the stage often omitted by acquirors – the commercial due diligence process – onto pricing and deal structures. Successful acquisitions rarely happen by chance; they are planned, and executed with great care and precision. The Acquisition Approvals Model will show you how.

The disposal process is based on a totally different mindset from the acquisition process.

A well advised vendor will conduct a covert controlled auction involving many buyers to achieve the most attractive deal. An acquiror will want a one-to-one deal with a vendor.

Again, to achieve an attractive price for a business when selling requires careful planning and execution. **The Covert Controlled Auction Model** is the rigorous route map which delivers attractive deals for vendors.

The model is explained in a stage-by-stage fashion including practical tips for grooming businesses prior to sale. Following the style of seminars presented by the author, the text includes anecdotal evidence to illustrate the principles discussed.

The first chapter of each part acts as an executive summary.

part one
acquisitions

The Acquisition Approvals Model

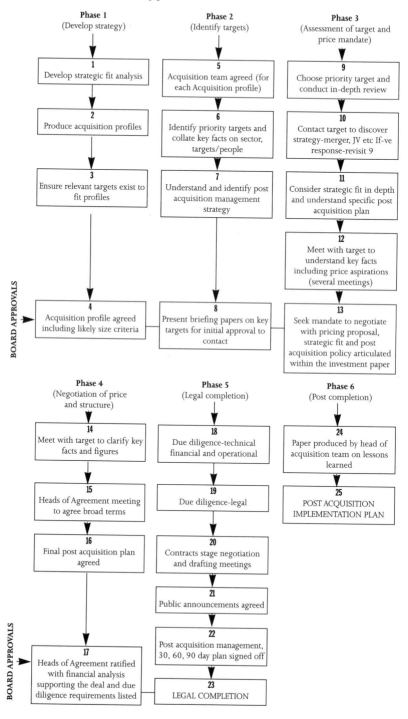

Phase 1
(Develop strategy)

1
Develop strategic fit analysis

2
Produce acquisition profiles

3
Ensure relevant targets exist to fit profiles

4
Acquisition profile agreed including likely size criteria

Phase 2
(Identify targets)

5
Acquisition team agreed (for each Acquisition profile)

6
Identify priority targets and collate key facts on sector, targets/people

7
Understand and identify post acquisition management strategy

8
Present briefing papers on key targets for initial approval to contact

Phase 3
(Assessment of target and price mandate)

9
Choose priority target and conduct in-depth review

10
Contact target to discover strategy-merger, JV etc If-ve response-revisit 9

11
Consider strategic fit in depth and understand specific post acquisition plan

12
Meet with target to understand key facts including price aspirations (several meetings)

13
Seek mandate to negotiate with pricing proposal, strategic fit and post acquisition policy articulated within the investment paper

BOARD APPROVALS

Phase 4
(Negotiation of price and structure)

14
Meet with target to clarify key facts and figures

15
Heads of Agreement meeting to agree broad terms

16
Final post acquisition plan agreed

17
Heads of Agreement ratified with financial analysis supporting the deal and due diligence requirements listed

Phase 5
(Legal completion)

18
Due diligence-technical financial and operational

19
Due diligence-legal

20
Contracts stage negotiation and drafting meetings

21
Public announcements agreed

22
Post acquisition management, 30, 60, 90 day plan signed off

23
LEGAL COMPLETION

Phase 6
(Post completion)

24
Paper produced by head of acquisition team on lessons learned

25
POST ACQUISITION IMPLEMENTATION PLAN

BOARD APPROVALS

The Acquisition Approvals Model

It should not be surprising that many acquisitions are a failure in the eyes of acquirors. Poor post acquisition strategies, the attitude of vendor management, inappropriate financial structuring of the deal or just bad pricing are some of the reasons given by the research.

Perhaps the reason for failure is much simpler than this: executives charged with implementing acquisition strategies have never done it before, and receive little specific guidance from the Group Board on a route map for success.

The route map in question is illustrated opposite. The map demonstrates, through a comprehensive logical set of stages, how to execute acquisitions. They do not need to be fickle, opportunistic and ego driven transactions with little science or rigour supporting them.

The importance of this model should not be underestimated. To mobilise a large group, to move all subsidiaries in the same overall direction using acquisitions is not easy.

The model allows the Group Board to sign off the best way forward at critical decision points.

This approvals process forces the acquisition team to present the logic and commercial rationale of the deal to the Group Board in measured stages. This forces strategy to the top of the agenda before price. It forces post acquisition management to be factored into the deal to ensure that the precise structure of the transaction is fit for the purpose – for example, because the vendor is often vital to the success of the transaction it may be appropriate to construct an earn-out deal.

The Acquisition Approvals Model breaks down into 6 distinct phases.

Phase I – Developing the strategy

First, the group must have an overall strategic vision. This top down strategy will be the back-cloth for the subsidiaries' organic and acquisition-led growth including research and development, joint ventures etc.

This has to be linked to a bottom up strategy at subsidiary level. Developing a growth strategy at subsidiary level is often relegated to a few weeks of the annual budget cycle. This is not the definition understood by ambitious Group Board members or subsidiary managing directors. The process is ongoing and constantly being reviewed to justify its relevance.

In this latter environment subsidiaries need to develop acquisition strategies which deliver the Group Board's vision of the future. Of course the breadth and comprehensiveness of this exercise will vary depending on the circumstances.

For example, a venture capital backed management buy-out company in say telecommunications distribution may have a clear short term aim to acquire half a dozen competitor or complementary service companies, the aim being to conduct a trade sale through a covert auction (Part 2 of this book) in three to five years' time.

However, a large quoted corporation will have a much wider remit on acquisitions covering many activities worldwide.

4

Whatever the specifics of the acquiring group it is imperative to have an agreed strategic direction from which flows relevant Acquisition Profiles. These are one to two page summaries highlighting the characteristics of the desired acquisition targets.

The Acquisition Profiles should be tested at an early stage to ensure that relevant targets exist.

These profiles can then be signed off by the Group Board, thus linking the top down view of growth sponsored by the Board with the ownership and commitment of the subsidiary managing directors and their teams.

These are discussed in more detail in the next Chapter.

Phase II – Identification of targets

This second phase of the process moves the acquiror from the theory of strategic direction to the practical deliverable of relevant targets and how they might fit within the group.

The facility to seek and find relevant targets around the globe has never been easier. Specific techniques are examined later in Chapter 3.

The acquisition search will produce many targets which may fit the strategic requirements of the group. Even at this early stage it is worth considering how these targets will be run, post acquisition. This work can then be honed into an investment paper for the Board, listing priority targets, their basic activities with financial background and their outline fit with the group.

Phase III – Assessment of target and price

Once the Board has approved a range of targets worth contacting, the priority target is now approached. A private company should be contacted by telephoning the majority shareholder or, if the target is a subsidiary of a listed group, the Chief Executive of the group.

The homework done in Phase II will stand acquirors in good stead for this call. A negative response should be followed up with a written explanation of the background to the call and a confirmation of the acquiror's enthusiasm for a meeting if circumstances change.

The priority list needs to be contacted until a positive response is obtained. Acquirors must develop a rigorous checklist of financial, operational and personnel facts and figures to be collated. This specific part of the process is called commercial due diligence. Rigorous attention to detail in understanding the target sector, the target itself and the key people within the target will allow acquirors to value the worth of the target to them. An acquiror's valuation of a company should be based on a sound, deliverable post acquisition strategy not the price aspiration of the vendor. Pricing unquoted companies is explored in detail in Chapter 8, Valuation and pricing tips.

An investment paper should now be written as a conclusion to Phase III of the approvals process. This paper will summarise the fit of the target with the Group, the proposed post acquisition strategy and the suggested pricing range and deal structure. In other words, a well thought through request for a price mandate to take into the next stage – Phase IV Negotiation of Price and Structure.

Phase IV — Negotiation of price and structure

The specific tactics under which price is delivered and negotiated will vary depending on whether an auction is being run by the vendor or, preferably from the acquiror's perspective, the vendor has been manoeuvred into a one to one scenario. These tactics are discussed in detail within Chapters 9 and 10 covering deal structures and negotiation. The end result, whatever the circumstances, will be the same — an agreement that a deal has been struck subject to contract and due diligence (not to be confused with commercial due diligence). This document, summarising the deal, is called the Heads of Agreement.

Armed with this document, signed off by both sides, the acquiror can revisit the Post Acquisition Plan, fine tune the detail and finally seek a ratification of the deal by the Group Board as a conclusion to Phase IV.

Phase V — Legal completion

The penultimate phase commences with the due diligence exercise — the verification of key facts and figures on the target. This will be both an accounting verification and a legal audit. This is an important opportunity for the acquiror to look closely on site at the books of account, the forecasts, the people, the legal documents, titles to property, patents, copyrights etc. A full checklist is provided in Appendix III.

Assuming a satisfactory due diligence phase, the acquiror often issues the sale and purchase contract although in trade sales from the public sector it is common for the vendor to issue the contract. The contracts are then negotiated between the parties, and there are some practical tips on this area for non-lawyers in Chapter 11.

The acquiror must continue to consider the post acquisition management agenda in these final stages of the deal. The first 30-90 day period post completion is critical to the long term success of the acquisition.

First impressions are important and therefore public announcements on the deal should be carefully considered. Both parties should approve the specific words and, of course, public announcements are an opportunity to sell the deal to all staff who have been unaware of the deal to date.

Phase VI – Post completion

The post acquisition plan needs to be implemented. Payroll, administration, sales tactics, warehousing rationalisation, accounting systems – the list is endless. A suggested plan of attack is explained in Chapter 7. Don't forget every acquisition is a learning opportunity for the rest of the Group. The head of the Acquisition Team should prepare a detailed report on lessons learned, for other key managers.

The Acquisition Approvals Procedure has been explained in outline. It is now time to consider in more detail the phases noted above. First, the Strategic Review is considered.

The Acquisition Approvals Model

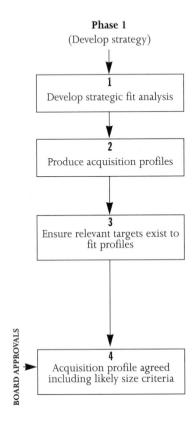

The strategic review

2

The strategic review of a business can take many forms but should include a detailed review of markets and the companies within those markets. An examination is required of the potential future development of your business within the changing map of the sector.

Establish your business segments

What business am I in? This may seem obvious but it is necessary to answer this question if acquisitions are to be contemplated by the group. Historical loyalties must be put to one side to allow an objective review of the business segments which will deliver shareholder value in the future.

Reckitt & Colman's move out of mustard, The Thomson Corporation's move out of regional newspapers and John Waddington's move out of games are good examples of large groups focusing on relevant business segments to deliver shareholder value.

Groups need to groom themselves for acquisition just as much as companies for sale may need to groom themselves prior to embarking on a trade sale.

Growth trends

Large groups must think through pan-global strategies for growth. It may be comforting to have a 30% market share of a UK market but if that represents a tiny percentage of the European or global market then the group should consider their options for growth carefully. Quality strategic thinking should encompass the potential growth strategy of existing businesses given the worldwide trends in global markets.

Of course for smaller groups an acquisition strategy centred around growing a significant UK market share may be more realistic and profitable than a strategy that looks overseas for expansion with limited management resources to execute it.

Environmental factors, new or projected legislation and customer developments may all be factors which will affect the group's thinking on the best way forward.

Acquisitions should only be contemplated when the issues surrounding the target market have been understood.

New segments

One area where acquisitions can transform the prospects of a group is diversification. It could be a telecoms business expanding their product range into new product segments or a valve manufacturer moving into other flow control products or a media company expanding their products into new technologies or industrial segments.

Has the strategic review uncovered the new areas of growth? The speed and effectiveness of an acquisition can far out-weigh the lower cost and safety of organic growth.

Specific analytical tools at your disposal to analyse markets and trends are discussed in Chapter 4.

Alternatives to acquisition growth

The strategic review should also unveil the alternatives to acquisition growth. Joint ventures (JV), operating contracts, franchising, trading relationships, new product development, minority stake investments and outsourcing are all outside the scope of this book but should all be considered.

The joint venture route is sometimes the only tool at your disposal to achieve growth. The recently announced Matra BAe Dynamics joint venture is a good example of a growth strategy for both partners where presumably acquisition wasn't possible. The JV will turnover £1bn and will employ 6,000 people.

Another recent example is Cookson Matthey Ceramics. The attempt to marry the Cookson industrial materials group with Johnson Matthey, the precious metals and engineering technology company, showed up deep differences in management style and culture. The industrial logic behind the joint venture has, however, overcome the tension.

Alternatively, rather than acquire 100% of a business, acquirors should consider the acquisition of a minority stake. British Airways' recent announcement of the sale of a minority stake in its engineering business represents an exciting opportunity for a relevant group. The issue to be agreed up front, as with all equity investments of this nature including joint ventures, is the divorce settlement. How is the acquiring group eventually to take control?

The benefits of an acquisition may sometimes be achieved more effectively through an operating contract to run the asset rather than own it. The recently floated MacDonald group of hotels built up a strong brand name in a short space of time through successful management contracts as well as selective acquisitions.

Manpower and Bodyshop are two successful examples of franchising being used to develop a group as an alternative to acquisitions.

If the objective is purely to secure better margins within a sector, a safer route may be to join a buying consortium. The commercial stationery market contains examples of companies benefiting from keen purchasing by being part of a much larger consortium.

New product development is not a technique solely for manufacturers but an area of importance to service companies. The speed of delivery to the market place of a new innovative service can be impressive. Acquisitions may not be possible in a new innovative product or service area.

Outsourcing of non-core services is a growing trend both within the public and private sector. Service businesses should consider all possible outsourcing opportunities at the same time as acquisitions. A good quality outsourcing contract can often deliver a better quality earnings stream than the acquisition of a target company.

Players in service sectors such as logistics, project management, IT and building maintenance should all be actively looking for outsourcing contracts from relevant large private and public sector organisations.

However, assuming that acquisitions are to form a major element in the group's growth strategy, the key is to produce deliverable acquisition profiles. These are the shopping lists describing the ideal target.

Acquisition profiles

One of the most important outputs from a company's regular strategic review should be a list of relevant acquisition priorities.

Acquirors may find it helpful to formalise their priorities using an acquisition profile.

No Name plc – European mergers and acquisitions criteria

Business profile   Complementary to No Name's existing interests in electrical products, fluid control and industrial services, for commercial and industrial applications.

Products principally associated with local distribution of energy, gases and fluids rather than extraction, generation and transmission.

Activities   Low/medium voltage circuit protection and control devices (under 1000 volts) including miniature circuit breakers, residual current breakers, moulded case circuit breakers, fusegear.

Motor control equipment (e.g. contractors, overload relays, variable speed controllers)

Wiring accessories, including plugs, sockets and switches.

Technology   Medium and stable technology manufacturing and services. No Name generally avoids markets dependent upon rapidly changing or 'leading edge' technologies.

Strong proprietary technology and strong design skills.

15

Market position	Good brand names, strong market share, broad customer base and well established routes to market – often through distributors.
	Strong aftermarket/replacement market potential.
Manufacturing	Manufacturers of finished products, but not complete systems. No Name is a manufacturer, not a contractor, and generally prefers to avoid turnkey projects.
Geography	Principal EU members; Germany, France, UK, possibly Spain, Italy, Benelux, and non EU states.
Financial	Profitable businesses. Sales probably in excess of £5m – £10m for existing business areas, and £20m for new business areas.
Management	Competent management team which No Name would expect to retain to develop the business.
Ownership	Probably family owned, or a non-core subsidiary of a larger group. Joint venture or minority participation may be considered, on the basis of control eventually moving to No Name within an agreed period.

The profile forces acquirors to prioritise their ideas and to articulate their thoughts in sufficient detail to find relevant targets.

Two specific tips on producing profiles are: firstly, have vision to your strategy not necessarily just bolt on acquisitions; secondly, keep the profiles short and sharp – no more than two pages of A4.

The Acquisition Approvals Model

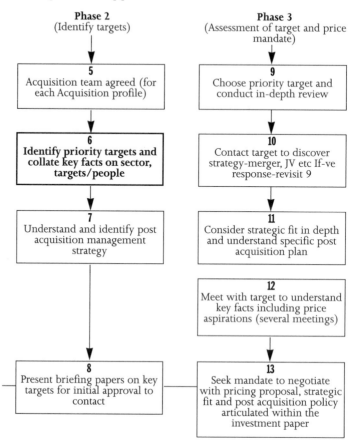

Phase 2
(Identify targets)

Phase 3
(Assessment of target and price mandate)

5
Acquisition team agreed (for each Acquisition profile)

9
Choose priority target and conduct in-depth review

6
Identify priority targets and collate key facts on sector, targets/people

10
Contact target to discover strategy-merger, JV etc If-ve response-revisit 9

7
Understand and identify post acquisition management strategy

11
Consider strategic fit in depth and understand specific post acquisition plan

12
Meet with target to understand key facts including price aspirations (several meetings)

8
Present briefing papers on key targets for initial approval to contact

13
Seek mandate to negotiate with pricing proposal, strategic fit and post acquisition policy articulated within the investment paper

How to find targets

3

Background

The reason many acquisitions fail, according to most research studies, is the lack of quality research done by the acquiror prior to completion.

It is the author's opinion, confirmed by recent research studies, that the important stage of commercial due diligence (including search) is poorly done by many acquirors prior to completing an acquisition. This leads to badly priced and structured deals and a poorly conceived post acquisition management strategy.

The following four chapters of the book, therefore, highlight the key techniques for reducing the risks from acquisitions by explaining the following commercial due diligence techniques:

1   how to find attractive vendors in the UK;

2   research tools to allow an assessment of market sector;

3   a rigorous route map for discovering the key facts and figures on the target; and

4   methods to discover key facts on the people.

First we look at techniques to find relevant targets which is the key to closing attractive deals for acquirors.

The practical techniques that can be effective are as follows:

1   knowledge within the business;

2   advertising;

3   communicating the acquisition profile; and

4   desk research.

These techniques are explained in detail below with real life examples to illustrate the principles.

Knowledge within the business

It is often surprising the range of acquisition ideas that can be generated from internal resources.

A **non-executive** director of a buildings supplies business was able to identify new products ideas from his knowledge of the market which complemented the existing catalogue.

Buyers, sales staff and technical staff if properly briefed are all capable of producing relevant ideas. Staff on the ground hear of opportunities long before the Group Board, especially when a target may be in difficulty where an early warning would be helpful.

Understanding the **needs of the customer** can lead to complementary skills or products being identified for possible acquisition. The Capita Group Plc and Serco Group Plc are good examples of initially small businesses which have grown rapidly by addressing the needs of customers. Both have diversified by acquisition and in the process filled product/service gaps to existing customers. In Capita's case the acquisition of Beard Dove, a wide ranging consultancy to the construction industry, has allowed Capita to satisfy the needs of a range of existing private and public sector clients whilst adding new clients to the Group's portfolio.

It may not be relevant for all acquirors, but on-site visits to customer factories or at the point of sale if products are retailed or trade fairs can all generate quality acquisition ideas to be followed up.

The point being, for companies which are on the acquisition trail, that there seems little downside to alerting internal staff to your priorities. This, of course, is a good example of why acquisitions are not the opposite of disposals. Don't alert your staff of your priorities when selling businesses (unless a public auction is envisaged)!

Advertising

As noted above, searching for vendors in the UK can be effective through a range of techniques. Advertising your requirements should be considered as a low cost device which may put you in touch with an attractive target.

The Business Wanted section of the Financial Times, which is published on Tuesdays, is probably the most effective medium.

Tips for a good advert include:

- keep it as specific as possible (a wide ranging advert generates irrelevant replies); and

- give names and phone numbers – vendors often don't give written responses.

It is worth noting that acquirors receiving an attractive response to an advert gain an immediate psychological advantage – the vendor presumably wants to sell.

BUSINESS WANTED

Specialist Technical Recruitment

Our Client is a successful UK based private company in the staffing services sector. It has a turnover of approximately £50m and the backing of a major institution. The company's aim is to develop the best technical recruitment business in Europe.

Target Criteria

- Activities: contract recruitment supplying specialist technical personnel to e.g. the IT, Engineering, Transport, Telecoms, Offshore or Construction sectors.

- Pre-tax profits £100k to £1 million.

- Vendor management willing to stay to develop the business.

- Probably located in the UK but businesses based in the Netherlands, France or Germany would also be attractive.

Please telephone, fax or write to Ian Smith or Kevin Jewell at Capita Corporate Finance.

Tel: 0171 799 1525 • Fax: 0171 233 1398

Capita Corporate Finance Limited
61-71 Victoria Street • Westminster • London SW1H 0XA

CAPITA
CORPORATE FINANCE

In addition to the above, trade press should be considered. However, often in trade sector magazines there is no obvious section for Business Wanted adverts and therefore these adverts often produce poor responses.

Acquisitions Monthly, the specialist magazine for the mergers and acquisitions industry, features a section on companies on the acquisition trail.

Of course, there are downsides for those listed groups communicating their acquisition requirements to a wider audience. Firstly, expectation will be built up in the City that the group will be closing deals and secondly, it may lift vendors' aspirations on price prior to initial contact. Therefore, so far as timing is concerned, acquirors should not promise to deliver in the current year but merely state that acquisitions will be considered on merit as they arise. Regarding price, practised acquirors who make their requirements widely known do not generally overpay.

Communicating the acquisition profile

Communicating your acquisition shopping list should improve the likelihood of finding attractive targets. Of course, like any good wanted poster, acquirors should be ready to offer rewards or 'finders fees' to intermediaries introducing quality vendors.

Acquirors should establish that, if rewards are to be paid (probably around 1% to 2% of the consideration), the intermediary receiving the commission is not also being paid by the vendors.

Effective communication should involve letting corporate finance advisors know your priorities e.g. merchant banks, corporate finance specialists and large accountancy practices as well as large legal practices. It is important to make regional offices of large advisory companies aware of your requirements.

Vendors can also be alerted to your appetite for acquisitions by using the Annual Accounts to reinforce the acquisition priorities or within an article on the interim or annual results.

Desk research

How to find targets

In desk research one of the main determinants of success is a good knowledge of information sources and, unfortunately, a thorough evaluative knowledge of the sources only comes with time and experience.

Directories – hard copy

Hard copy print directories of UK company information fall into two broad categories:

1   General – e.g. Kompass, Kellys, Key British Enterprises (KBE) and Macmillans' Unquoted Companies.

Several of these are multi-volume works with listings arranged alphabetically, geographically, by turnover, by employment numbers and (most importantly for the issue in hand) by product within a Standard Industrial Classification (SIC) – type arrangement. For our purpose – the identification of potential target companies by specific business activity – Kompass remains the premier source among the print directories for the precision of searching it allows the user.

2   Sector specific e.g. Machinery Buyers Guide, Engineer Buyers Guide

Unfortunately, these are not widely available. To identify the directories specific to your area of interest, it is necessary to consult some tertiary sources. Two of the most useful ones in this case are Current British Directories and Croner's A-Z of Business Information Sources. It is important with trade-specific company directories to take note of the level of coverage. This can vary considerably and you may find yourself getting a very incomplete picture of the players in a sector. Alternatively, trade associations relevant to the industry under investigation may be able to help with identifying company directories in their industry. These associations themselves can be located using two other tertiary sources – the Directory of British Associations (DBA) and the Aslib Directory of Information Sources in the UK. Bodies listed in the DBA may vary in their ability and willingness to help you but organisations listed in the Aslib Directory can at least be guaranteed to possess some form of library or information resource which should be able to provide some guidance.

Electronic databases

A search to find acquisition targets is an instance where database searching is not just quicker and likely to yield more up-to-date information than a traditional trawl through printed directories but is likely to be more cost efficient. In a database search it is possible to be very precise about criteria and combine several together in a single search e.g. SIC code, turnover, profit, location etc. In addition, the resulting output can be produced in a tailored format and presented in a spreadsheet, for example.

The names of the main publishers of company information databases have a familiar ring to anyone who has an acquaintance with the leading print directories. Kompass, ICC, Dun & Bradstreet and Jordans all produce company information databases either on-line or as CD-ROMs, direct or via hosts.

Most databases are accessed through host systems which allow the user to interrogate a suite of databases produced by different publishers using one single command language. Many databases are available from more than one host. In addition some publishers are also hosts. An example is company information from ICC, available via Dialog and Datastar as just

25

one file among the hundreds which they host but also available direct from ICC.

The two main competing CD-ROM company information sources are FAME (Financial Analysis Made Easy) published by Bureau van Dijk using data supplied by Jordans and OneSource which obtains its data from ICC. Reed has also entered this market with Kompass on CD. Each of these has a broadly equivalent on-line database. Besides allowing a much more sophisticated approach to searching, the on-line and CD-ROM versions of these directories contain far more records and the data is more timely. On-line databases are in a state of continual revision and a CD-ROM subscriber usually receives an updated disc at least once a month depending on the publisher.

Buying help – using information brokers and intermediaries

Access to information resources is not a problem for large and medium-sized companies with information departments because information professionals are on hand to execute the searches for the ultimate user or provide advice and training on networked end-user systems. For those without this level of research support, many public libraries, research institutes, professional bodies and specialist information brokers have established fee-based services, offering among other facilities, database searching. Examples in the London-area include:

1   Public libraries like Westminster Reference Library with its Information for Business unit and the City Business Library whose bolt-on fee-based business service is called Business Information Focus.

2   Professional research bodies for specific industries like the Leatherhead Food Research Association.

3   The British Library itself, which has a Business Information Service based at the Science Reference Information Service.

4   Newspapers – many newspapers have libraries for internal use but the Financial Times also has the Financial Times Research Centre which carries out research for outsiders.

5   Academic institutions like the London Business School.

Most of these, and similar independent information brokers, calculate their fees from two components: their time and the cost of retrieving the information. This can be the most cost-efficient method of accessing information because the user buys not just expertise in searching, knowledge of the command languages etc but the researcher's knowledge of the sources.

There are some types of information which are virtually impossible to obtain except from a database (the research reports of stockbrokers' analysts are an example) but most of the data, be it accounts, statistics, articles or whatever is still published in another format, usually printed hard copy. In choosing the means for accessing particular information, it is necessary to weigh up a number of factors and assess your own priorities.

1   How urgently is the information required?

2   What skills are needed to retrieve the data in its different formats?

3   In which forms is the material available?

4   What is the budget for the exercise?

5   Is it important to have the output in a special format?

Once these questions have been answered, it may become clear that electronic sources can be side-stepped or that part of the research could be more efficiently subcontracted.

Buying help – using specialist acquisition advisors

Quality acquisition advisors, e.g. merchant banks, large accountancy practices and corporate finance boutiques, will contain research departments focused on mergers and acquisitions.

The rules of engagement in using these advisors are:

1 Expect to pay £5k to £10k per sector for acquisition target search work.

2 Sector research work needs to be specified and a maximum budget set.

3 Further work beyond research i.e. valuation, deal structuring and negotiation is obviously a core service of these advisors and should be separately quoted.

4 A success fee or bonus will be payable if a deal is completed from targets identified.

Tips for choosing acquisition advisors regarding research:

1 Meet the researcher who will do the work.

2 Ask them to explain their network of contacts they will use.

3 Ask them to explain how they will conduct the research i.e. what databases they will access.

4 Agree timescales for delivery of relevant targets per sector – normally this should be within six weeks.

The Acquisition Approvals Model

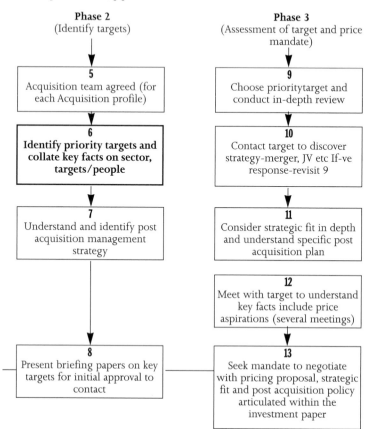

Phase 2
(Identify targets)

Phase 3
(Assessment of target and price mandate)

5 Acquisition team agreed (for each Acquisition profile)	**9** Choose prioritytarget and conduct in-depth review
6 **Identify priority targets and collate key facts on sector, targets/people**	**10** Contact target to discover strategy-merger, JV etc If-ve response-revisit 9
7 Understand and identify post acquisition management strategy	**11** Consider strategic fit in depth and understand specific post acquisition plan
	12 Meet with target to understand key facts include price aspirations (several meetings)
8 Present briefing papers on key targets for initial approval to contact	**13** Seek mandate to negotiate with pricing proposal, strategic fit and post acquisition policy articulated within the investment paper

Understanding the sector

4

Clearly, a company implementing a diversification strategy will want to understand possible new sectors as well as it can. However the occasion of any acquisition is an opportunity to step back from the fray and review a particular industry; the wider social, economic and political factors bearing on its performance and future, and the position and performance of the players, particularly the potential targets and even of the acquiror itself. How else will acquirors recognise rarity value!

Thefore this chapter reviews various techniques to assist acqrurors understand the map of the sector. The following techniques are explained:

1 Quick and easy method – The Market Research Report
2 The detailed method -   **a) Introduction to desk research**
                                          b) Understanding broad economic context
                                          c) Using newspapers and journals
                                          d) Using government statistics
                                          e) Access to legislation and regulations
                                          f) Investment analysts/brokers research
                                          g) Acquisition databases

Quick and easy method – the market research report

The one-stop solution to a sector review is to buy a market research study. Potentially this will give you the big picture in one document – the macro economic statistics, social and lifestyle changes, legislative pressures shaping the industry etc and the situation in the specific market – size, growth prospects, niches, consumer profiles, players, market shares etc. There are estimated to be about 30,000 market research reports in print. The tertiary sources in this area to help you track down those relevant to your particular subject of enquiry include:

1   Findex

2   MarketSearch

3   Marketing Surveys Index

4   Market Research Locator (CD version of Findex produced by Knight-Ridder)

Most business libraries and many larger general public libraries have one or all of these in stock. Again the DBA and the Aslib Directory can give guidance on trade associations and research bodies which should know of publishers producing reports on their sector. There are many comparatively small producers covering discrete sectors, however the main general publishers of market research include:

1   Euromonitor

2   Mintel

3   Datamonitor

4   Economist Intelligence Unit

5   Frost & Sullivan

6   ICC Keynote

Most of their output examines fairly broad consumer sectors because these are the products most often studied in depth by advertising agencies and marketing organisations (who represent the best customers for these reports). They are available in printed hard copy (some of those at the cheaper end of the scale, e.g. Keynote, are taken by business libraries) or can be accessed in electronic format. A British Library publication *Market Research: a guide to British Library holdings* lists those held by the BL. The publishers mentioned above (and others besides) have made their reports available via the main on-line hosts e.g. *Knight-Ridder (Dialog/Datastar)*, *FT Profile* and *MAID*. Even more than usual, it is very easy to run up a large bill when searching these hosts for market research because the relevant files attract a premium charge. For example via the FT Profile host, printed extracts from a Mintel report are charged at the rate of £0.30 per line (1996 price). Display costs are much lower on MAID but the user is charged an annual subscription fee of £5,950 (1996 price). Increasingly, CD-ROM is becoming an option too, although timeliness is an issue with this kind of information in the CD-ROM format. Again, *ICC Keynote* reports are an example. The CD-ROM Directory is a good place to check for other possibilities.

Even though these on-line files often carry a premium charge and are among the most expensive databases which the mainstream hosts offer, searching them on-line can still be the most cost-efficient method because it is possible to extract only the sections, chapters, tables etc of direct interest instead of purchasing the entire study, only parts of which may be of direct relevance to the exercise in hand.

In addition to full reports there are also a number of market research journals which usually carry several shorter reviews of a number of markets or products in each issue. Examples include *Mintel Market Intelligence* and *Retail Business*.

The detailed method

If a report, recently produced and not too expensive, exists for your sector of interest, then it represents an easy, cost-effective solution but invariably this is not the case. The sector of interest may be too niche or cut across recognised markets. Available reports may be out-of-date or too expensive (many cost thousands of pounds) and be unavailable even from business libraries and hence rule themselves out as a viable source. Remember that market research reports can only give an approximate indication of an industry in general and also sometimes extrapolate quite small sample surveys to make general assumptions about a whole industry – this is especially true with forecasts. Although some of the material presented in market research reports comes from surveys which the companies themselves have carried out and collated, much of it is synthesised and analysed data extracted from primary sources in the public domain e.g. government statistics, which has then been reproduced in a more accessible form. Although an individual researcher will not be able to bring to bear the resources of a market research company, it is nonetheless possible to gather a large amount of market, sector and product information to create your own analytical picture of an industry of interest. If one starts at the broadest level, you might first want to survey the overall general social and economic context in which the potential target companies are operating. This is essential when making an acquisition overseas and this is discussed in Chapter 12 but in this chapter we focus on the sources available for desk research supporting the acquisition of a UK business. In the home market an analysis of the broad socio-economic context may be considered an unnecessary preliminary to retrieving information for an economic analysis of the specific sector. However, this kind of exercise is an opportunity to go beyond a brief scanning of the press, to analyse factors driving change in the UK economy and society which may impinge on the performance of an industry or business.

The detailed method – understanding the broad economic context

Ultimately the key source for most macro economic data is the Central Statistical Office (CSO) of the UK Government. Although its output has been curtailed somewhat in recent years, it still produces numerous series of statistics. To navigate through this mass of information, it is necessary to consult another tertiary source, the Guide to Official Statistics – unfortunately not updated for several years. Two summary compilations deserve special mention – the Annual Abstract of Statistics and Economic Trends. Both bring together data from other CSO series and it is often enough just to consult these unless a very detailed picture is required. Other useful titles from the CSO stable are Regional Trends, General Household Survey, Social Trends, Family Expenditure Survey and UK National Accounts (Blue Book). All of these are widely available from larger public libraries. Generally speaking Government statistics are not easily digestible and, particularly if you do not need to prepare a thorough and detailed analysis, it may be enough to use the financial press for this information. The quality daily newspapers and weeklies, like the Economist, are the obvious sources in this respect. As explained below, databases make searching across a range of newspapers and journals so much easier than attempting to find the same material in hard copy.

The detailed method – using newspapers and journals

The general level of prosperity and certain kinds of social change can have a bearing on the success of a product or market but specific products can be affected by the performance of the wider sector-e.g. DIY warehouse retailing is intricately tied up with the health of the housing market. Moreover the consuming sector needs to be examined as well as the producing one.

Taking an example from the housing sector: clearly to evaluate the state of the market for bricks, it is necessary to understand the general state of

35

the construction industry. It is at this broad sector level that market research reports can be most valuable but even without them it is possible to build up a full picture of a sector.

General and trade press – The general press is an especially good place to start a search on a sector which is largely unknown to you, particularly if it employs an unfamiliar technology. Articles and surveys in the mainstream press will have been written for the general reader and hence provide a useful entree into strange territory. They may also refer to other potential sources of information when they, for example, report on a newly published survey or study.

The trade press is almost the only source for up-to-date in-depth information on very narrow subsectors of commercial markets. Trade journals can also put you in touch with other specialists in a given field or on occasion will make their own unpublished source material available. The best way to identify journals in a particular field, apart from contacting professional associations, is to consult a directory of serials with a classified listing. Examples include:

1 *Benns*

2 *PiMS*

3 *Willings*

The problem with trade journals, unlike mainstream newspapers and journals, is finding a location with a back file of the ones you are looking for. It is many years since a union list of all serials in the UK and their locations existed; similarly very few libraries still maintain cuttings files or subscribe to *McCarthy Cards*. The British Library publishes *Current Serials Received*, a source guide which many public libraries hold. It is not, though, a guide to the contents of journals. You need to know the bibliographic citation of the article required i.e. at least some of the following: title, author, journal name, the date of the issue, page numbers. Once you have verified that an article which you need appeared in a serial held by the British Library's Document Supply Centre, any library can order it, although delivery times can be long, stretching to weeks rather than days. Public libraries usually pass only a small proportion of the cost of this process on to the user.

Accessing newspapers and journals on-line

The main reason for the disappearance of cuttings files is that databases make the searching of newspapers and journals so much easier and more efficient:

1   It is possible to access hundreds of newspapers and journals in just a few minutes on one database.

2   On-line database searching allows the researcher a flexibility to combine several criteria in one search and look for keywords in the text rather than a narrow range of predetermined index terms.

3   Database searching can be interactive, it is possible to have a dialogue with a database, a search strategy can be amended on-line and immediately rerun.

4   Currency – even CD-ROM databases are far more up-to-date than printed indices.

5   Databases permit the long term monitoring of a company or sector using alerts or SDIs (Selective Dissemination of Information) – particularly valuable if you are 'stalking' a target and invariably less expensive than using a cuttings service.

The best guides for identifying the journals you are looking for are Full-text Journals On-line, The On-line Manual, Books & Periodicals On-line and Gale's Directory of On-line Databases.

The leading full-text databases of UK newspapers and mainstream non-specialist journals are:

1   *Textline* (available via a number of hosts).

2   *FT Profile* – a host with a suite of databases which include *McCarthy On-line*, the electronic version of the cards service.

In addition to these general trade journals' databases there are also databases which concentrate on journals in a specific industry. For example:

1   *The Paper Industry Research Association (PIRA)* has a database (on-line via the *Knight-Ridder* hosts) which focuses on the paper and packaging sector.

2   *The Rubber and Plastics Research Association (RAPRA)* maintains a similar database of sector journals (also on-line via the *Knight-Ridder* hosts).

However there are issues surrounding both the cost and the expertise required to use sources in this form which may rule out their use at present, except through intermediaries. Furthermore, despite the enormous gains of recent years which have seen thousands of newspapers, magazines, journals and serials put up on-line, many, particularly those concerned with niche businesses, remain available only in hard copy in the back files of professional associations, trade bodies and academic institutions.

The detailed method – using government statistics

Data collected, collated and published by the CSO is not just useful for developing a picture of the national macro-economic situation and trends. It can also help in building up an understanding of the size and structure of an industry or sector. The most useful for this purpose is the *Business Monitors* series. The publication of this has changed recently with some of the material (e.g. the manufacturers' updates, formerly the PAS and PQ series, now renamed UK Markets) available in formats other than just hard copy from the publishers, *Taylor Nelson*. However the census of production parts of the *Business Monitors* has remained unchanged and the summary issues, PA1002 and PA1003 which analyse UK business by size, industrial classification and location are particularly helpful in this kind of sector analysis. The long-time series with several years' data, are especially valuable for tracking trends. Business Monitors are often available from public libraries which have subscriptions to HMSO publications. Another often overlooked source of government-produced sector information is the Monopolies & Mergers Commission. Its reports provide in-depth studies of the industries it is asked to investigate for monopolistic or restrictive practices.

The detailed method – access to legislation and regulations

Data produced by governments and pan-national governmental agencies can aid the process of understanding a sector and the companies in it. Governments are also the instrument of legislative and regulatory change which frequently have profound repercussions for the fortunes of entire industrial sectors. The deregulation of markets across the globe has acted as a terrific stimulus in many sectors and in some cases has created entirely new private sector industries. To take another example, increased concern for the physical environment and the impact of industrial activity on it has forced a fundamental change in some manufacturing techniques and led to the termination of others. For some businesses unable to meet the imposition of new costs from this source, changes like these have spelt oblivion, but for others they represent an opportunity. For the acquiror about to make an investment in a sector by buying a business, it is clearly crucial to avoid nasty surprises at a later stage and identify any legislative proposals which might materially affect the future prospects of the target and hence its future and present value.

A search of the relevant trade journals, in whatever format, should alert you to any proposed changes in UK legislation with significant potential ramifications for the industry under investigation. UK government proposals appear as Green or White Papers and subsequently as Bills if they are proceeded with and are published as Command Papers, House of Commons Papers and Bills by HMSO. As such they are easily available either from HMSO itself or from larger reference libraries.

European legislation is another matter. Like national legislation it may provoke discussion in the press, either general or trade. However, it is as well to go beyond this and check specific sources. Some European legislation has to be transposed into national law and hence passes through the stages which we identified above but some regulations have direct application. Directives come into force in the UK by Statutory Instrument, although the SI itself may not explain the Directive's provisions. Just as UK national legislation passes across a series of hurdles before taking its place on the Statute Book, so EU legislation passes through a number of stages; although the role of the European Parliament is less central to the process than the Westminster Parliament is in the UK model. What sources exist to identify regulations or directives at the proposal or consultation stage? How do you find a detailed description of the provisions of a directive which appears to have implications for the sector in which you are proposing to invest?

Some legislation sources to consider are:

1   **Libraries.** The European Commission's London office operates an
    Information Service. More usefully, several academic libraries have
    been designated European Documentation Centres (EDCs). Others,
    including Westminster Reference Library, have European
    Depository Library status. In addition European Information
    Centres designed to support business have been established in
    Chambers of Commerce under the auspices of the DTI and almost
    all local authorities have signed up to the Public Information Relay
    which provides European Commission information.

2   **CELEX.** A full-text on-line database of European Union treaties,
    agreements, legislation, preparatory documents etc. which enables

the enquiror to discover the status of any piece of proposed legislation. It can be accessed via the host's Data-Star and FT Profile.

3   **Context publications**. These include JUSTIS CELEX CD-ROM, a quarterly updated version of the CELEX on-line database containing the text of European legislation since 1952 and its companion disc JUSTIS Official Journal – C which can be used to identify and link proposed legislation (COMDOCs) and features the full text of all proposals since 1990.

4   **Directory of Legislation in Force**. Has the potential to be a useful source but at present the indexing is poor.

Investment analysts/brokers research

Like market research reports these can represent a useful short cut to an understanding of a sector. However there is a problem with access. It can be easy to identify a useful report, perhaps because its conclusions are discussed in a newspaper or journal article. Rarely, though, are such reports freely distributed to those not on the analysts' mailing lists. Invariably they are either completely unavailable or sold for large sums of money. However, there is an alternative approach; some houses allow their research output (usually the shorter, more superficial pieces which do not have a long-term value) to go onto databases after an embargo period (usually about two months) has passed. Suppliers of brokers' research in this form are:

1   *Investext*   –   available direct and via hosts.

2   *ICC*   –   available direct and via hosts.

3   *ARK*   –   a subsidiary of Investext which publishes brokers' research on the UK on CD-ROM.

Databases of brokers' research, like those for market research, carry a premium charge but do give the user the opportunity to search for relevant pieces from among the output of many houses and then subsequently, by selecting only those parts of the reports directly relevant to the task in hand, to buy only useful material. This can be the most cost-efficient way of accessing brokers' reports.

Acquisition databases

As part of a sector review in the context of a planned acquisition, it is useful to look at recent acquisition activity.

Firstly, the success or failure of comparable diversifications can provide warnings of possible pitfalls and secondly, it may give an indication of potential deal values.

Again, the general and trade press is a good source of news on mergers and acquisitions. Database searching represents the best way of accessing this information, not just because the enquiror can search across a whole range of sources simultaneously but because it is possible to focus precisely on articles about acquisitions in a defined sector during a particular time period. As more and more markets around the world have been liberalised and restrictions on take-overs eased, so the level of activity and the accompanying interest in the subject has increased. Specialist sources have grown up to inform this interest:

1   The premier journal in this area is *Acquisitions Monthly*.

2   *AMDATA* – the publishers of *Acquisitions Monthly* have used their data to construct a mergers and acquisitions database. This is not simply the text articles from the printed version on-line but rather a database of deals which can be accessed using a variety of criteria and displayed in varying levels of detail.

3   The Financial Times covers the subject in a similar way. Its M&A database is available on its own host *FT Profile* and via the *Knight-Ridder* host *Datastar*.

4   *Thomson Financial*, through their database division *IFR Securities Data*, make available, in addition to capital markets data, information on M&A deals.

All these publishers find themselves handicapped in the same way. It is often possible to find that a small private deal happened but pursuing the details of the transaction can be a fruitless task if the parties involved chose not to disclose them. This frustration can be reflected in the amount of blank space in the print out from these M&A databases.

Understanding the sector – conclusions

Therefore, given the above, there is no excuse for acquirors not to be well-informed on the dynamics of the specific sector. Remember, the need to test vendor's assertions on their marketplace will be paramount in later discussions and therefore homework done is rarely wasted.

We now examine recommended methods for investigating the target company.

The Acquisition Approvals Model

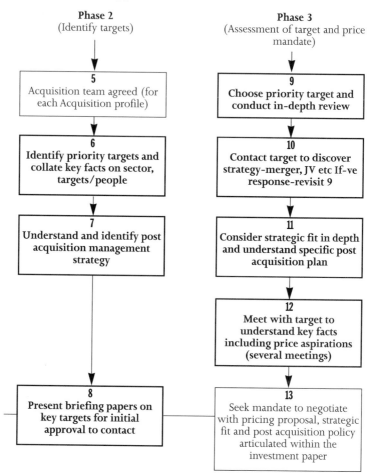

Phase 2
(Identify targets)

Phase 3
(Assessment of target and price mandate)

5
Acquisition team agreed (for each Acquisition profile)

9
Choose priority target and conduct in-depth review

6
Identify priority targets and collate key facts on sector, targets/people

10
Contact target to discover strategy-merger, JV etc If-ve response-revisit 9

7
Understand and identify post acquisition management strategy

11
Consider strategic fit in depth and understand specific post acquisition plan

12
Meet with target to understand key facts including price aspirations (several meetings)

8
Present briefing papers on key targets for initial approval to contact

13
Seek mandate to negotiate with pricing proposal, strategic fit and post acquisition policy articulated within the investment paper

Understanding the
target company

5

Understanding the target in this context means using public domain information and information supplied directly by the vendor.

For the purpose of desk research, public domain company information can be divided into financial and non-financial, the latter comprising information about products, techniques, technology, management practices etc.

This chapter is divided into:

1   Financial information – public domain.

2   Non-financial information – public domain.

3   Financial information – after successful approach to the vendor.

4   Non-financial information – after successful approach to the vendor.

Financial information – public domain

Primary sources

Almost all financial information on UK companies can ultimately be traced to the records of *Companies House* where all private limited and public limited companies are obliged to register and to file annual returns and accounts. Enforcement of these requirements has become more stringent over the last few years, so some financial data can usually be obtained on all registered companies. Concessions are made for 'small' and 'medium' sized companies which can file abbreviated accounts. For 'small' companies this means a modified balance sheet with some supporting notes. At present for financial disclosure purposes 'small' and 'medium' are defined as follows:

A company is 'small' if it meets at least **two** of the following criteria:

1   turnover <£2.8M

2   balance sheet total <£1.4M

3   employees <50 in number

To qualify as 'medium' sized, a company needs to meet at least **two** of the following requirements:

1   turnover <£11.2M

2   balance sheet total <£5.6M

3   employees <250

These criteria are adjusted periodically to take account of inflation.

Although these concessions are not helpful for research purposes, not all companies take advantage of them (full accounts have to be prepared for the shareholders anyway) and they do not, for example, apply to public limited companies or companies which are part of a group containing a plc.

Companies House is then the obvious primary source for company financial information. Agencies (ICC and Dun & Bradstreet among many others offer this service) will do a search for you or you can visit in person or use the telephone search service of Companies House itself. The cost depends on the method and speed of delivery. The annual reports of quoted companies are, of course, available without charge from the companies or their registrars or via the *Financial Times Annual Reports Service* which covers the majority of quoted companies.

Secondary sources

Alternatively, a researcher can go straight to secondary sources which use the Companies House filings as their main raw material but synthesise and analyse the raw data and re-present it in a form which makes it more useful for comparative purposes. If the object of the exercise is **to measure a company's performance against others** in the same sector, then moving straight on to the secondary sources will save a lot of time. Some of the leading suppliers in this field are:

1   ICC

2   *Jordans*

3   *Dun & Bradstreet*

4   *Infocheck*

5   CCN

ICC, which is also one of the companies which act as agents for obtaining hard copy or microfiche accounts from *Companies House*, maintains a database of UK companies' accounts (via *Knight-Ridder* hosts or direct), also supplied to *Bureau van Dijk* for their *Onesource* CD-ROMs.

In hard-copy, ICC are the publishers of the *ICC Business Ratio Reports* which contain a comparative analysis of the financial performance of the largest companies in a sector and the *ICC Financial Surveys* which bring together the basic accounts data for almost all companies in a sector (several thousand as opposed to the several hundred which a *Business Ratio* Report will cover).

The latter three in the list (*D&B*, *Infocheck* and *CCN*) not only abstract and interpret information which has been deposited at *Companies House* but also provide credit information including a rating. *Jordans* and *Kompass* also offer company information on CD-ROM. Print directories from some of the organisations mentioned above (*Dun & Bradstreet, Kompass*) are another alternative format but their limitations in this context are many e.g. fewer companies are covered, less data is available on each one etc.

Non-financial information – public domain

The financial performance of a target will of course affect its desirability but it is also at this stage of the acquisition process that the acquiror should examine in detail the company's activities and products, its competitive position, the market's perception of it and its shareholder base.

Main activities

We looked, at the outset, at the activities of companies in order to identify those which met the acquiror's criteria. At this more advanced stage, but still before the potential targets have been approached or any site visits are contemplated, it is necessary to go beyond the product analysis available from printed company directories or their electronic equivalents.

We have mentioned the general and trade press as a source for news on company activities. The local press is another possibility but access is a problem. Due to its commercial sensitivity, this information can be difficult to obtain but here again trade bodies and professional organisations can be worth contacting. They often publish their own information or at least maintain membership lists which seek to break down the constituent companies by activity. Some larger ones even maintain libraries of product information from their membership. Sometimes though this method will not yield results or not provide enough data on which to make a judgement, and an approach to the companies themselves is the only remaining solution. This is an instance where intermediaries can be particularly useful. They may be successful in obtaining product information by making a direct but unattributed approach to the companies under consideration.

Competitive position and market perception

If they have not already been set up, it is now advisable to establish alerts on databases which feature trade journals relevant to the sector and run them every few days. These will keep you up-to-date on developments – products, legislation, appointments, financial results etc and supplement the information gained at the earlier stage when gathering information on the sector and the target's position in the sector. Brokers' research is another useful source for an objective analysis of a company in relation to its sector.

Shareholding base

Both Thomson Financial, through CDA/Spectrum Sharewatch, and Jordans, with Jordanshare, offer services which detail the shareholders of quoted companies down to shareholdings of 0.15%. Although these can be invaluable if speed is the most important factor, ultimately this data is sourced from the companies' annual returns. If speed is not important or the company is not listed and especially if the returns have been obtained for financial analysis anyway, it is as well to go direct to the primary source, i.e. Companies House, either direct or via one of the agents mentioned above.

Financial information – after successful approach to the vendor

The above sources will assist the acquiror in building up an outline picture of the target. However a detailed review can only begin with the co-operation of the vendor. The following checklist needs to be investigated with the assistance of the vendor. This may take several meetings and the level of information you require will often have to be negotiated.

1   Aged debt analysis

2   Aged work in progress and stock analysis

3   Gross margin history

4   Material movements in overheads from year to year

5   Sales history and projections

6   Future cashflows

7   Salary costs for key employees

8   Owner benefits

9   Accounting policies understood and appropriate

10 Capital investment for expansion

11 Cost of refurbishment

12 PAYE/VAT history

The experience of many deals suggests that **debtors and stock/work in progress** are areas fraught with problems for the uninitiated acquiror. The simple fact is that material balances may not be collectable, and within private company balance sheets vendor management may have persuaded auditors not to restate balance sheet values downwards to reflect reality, due to the low net asset value in these balance sheets supporting bank debt.

Real life example — retentions

A mechanical and electrical sub-contractor appeared to have strong profit growth throughout the recession 1990-93. On closer inspection, retention monies in excess of £1 million were doubtful and subject to legal dispute. The original problem was not between the target vendor and his client the main contractor, but between the main contractor and his client. The main contractor had no chance of recovering his money and therefore the vendor target was being hopelessly optimistic.

Conclusion

If debts or work in progress are old, even though quality documentation and a strong legal case for recovery exists, as an acquiror, follow through the audit trail of the original transaction to establish whether the cash is likely to be collected.

A study of **gross margins** over several years should reveal whether sales are being won at any price, the competitive nature of the sector and the volume and yield drivers influencing the target's performance.

On reviewing **sales history and projections** it is important for an acquiror to identify one-off items which might distort historical trends.

Future cashflows should reveal the cash generative nature of the business and whether a refinancing may be required in the short to medium-term.

The need to understand the **cost base** is obvious, but, specifically in private companies, the subject of owner benefits can reveal significant cost savings. Find out the costs which will not continue post acquisition; the sponsorship of the son's rally career, the Spanish villa (sales office) costs, the second car for family members, the high level of personal expense accounts every month.

Misunderstood **accounting policies** can lead to a completely wrong picture of the target being assembled. Items treated as extraordinary or exceptional must be understood. Costs that have been capitalised must be broken down and reviewed through an acquiror's eyes to determine their true impact on the profit and loss account.

The need for material **capital investment** must be clarified, explained and options discussed.

Non-financial information – after successful approach to the vendor

Once contact has been made with the target, the key point is to build up a picture which confirms your post acquisition management strategy.

As mentioned above there is key financial data which you will investigate but don't forget the key operational areas once on site.

If an accurate post acquisition scenario is to be developed then key operational areas must be understood and compared with the acquiror's own business.

The following areas serve as a useful checklist on operational areas:

1 Details on premises

2 Vendor's assessment of competitors

3 Production capacity and efficiency

4 Distribution channels

5 Research and development of projects

6 Service contracts

7 Health and safety issues

8 Compatibility of culture and style

9 Environmental issues

These checklist points are examined in more detail below.

Under **premises**, acquirors must clarify whether all relevant buildings are owned by the company, as it is common for private company shareholders to own some or all of the premises from which the company trades. Are valuations up to date, or is the balance sheet overstated?

Although analysis should be conducted into the sector and the competitiveness of all the players within the sector, it is important for acquirors to understand the **vendor's assessment of its competitors**. It is likely that the vendor will have conducted a detailed review of the strengths and weaknesses of its competition in the market place.

An assessment of the vendor's **production capacity** will enable a meaningful assessment of post acquisition profits, and identify at an early stage crucial factors in integrating the target into the acquiring group.

Real life example – production capacity

A vendor presenting the financial case to the acquiror was careful to explain the unnecessary production units both in Ireland and the South of England. The former was sited there for tax reasons at the time and the latter site was a smaller, inefficient version of the buyer's larger site in the Midlands.

Conclusion

The acquiror was able to discuss in more detail the post acquisition integration of the business with his Board.

An understanding of **distribution channels** is also vital for the acquiror to build a complete picture. Several industries including steel, tyres and paper have consolidated over the years by manufacturers acquiring distribution outlets. By understanding the distribution channels in detail, acquirors will be able to assess the true value of owning the target and understand the necessary changes that will be required post acquisition.

Real life example – distribution channels

In considering distribution channels, branding and vertical integration must be considered e.g. acquirors must consider whether to impose their group name or retain the original brand. Prudential chose to brand their estate agents while Legal and General chose not to. Regarding vertical integration, a strong branded manufacturer branding a distributor with the same name is in danger of alienating all other distributors in the market-place.

Conclusion

Acquirors may be able to boost sales of their product/service by acquiring a distributor, but careful assessment is required of the effect on the vendor's business as well as the attitude of other distributors.

Research and development is not only the province of manufacturing companies. It should be just as relevant for a service company to continually research service gaps in the marketplace that it can serve e.g. new developments in media have included video advertisements on buses and in post offices.

It may seem odd to discuss under operational issues the detailed **service contracts of key managers**, but acquirors must assess at the earliest possible stage, the cost of rationalising the management team and, for those managers remaining with the business, the on going employment costs.

Assessing differences between the acquiror and the vendor regarding **culture** is difficult. However, if an acquiror ignores material differences, e.g. as between a large institution such as a regional electricity company and a vendor target in the contracting sector, there is a danger that post acquisition problems will arise and motivation and performance will suffer. Strategic fit cannot be solely focused around markets and financial numbers but must take into account the styles of the various management teams working closely together.

Finally, ignorance of **environmental issues** surrounding the vendor is likely to prove costly for even the most practised acquiror.

Therefore, having investigated three key areas for reducing an acquirors risk i.e.

- finding targets

- assessing sectors

- assessing targets

We now turn to the fourth and final method – understanding the people.

The Acquisition Approvals Model

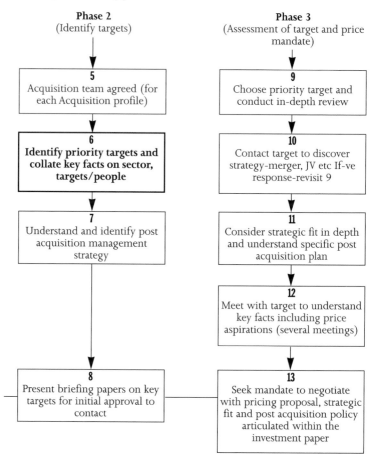

Phase 2
(Identify targets)

5
Acquisition team agreed (for each Acquisition profile)

6
Identify priority targets and collate key facts on sector, targets/people

7
Understand and identify post acquisition management strategy

8
Present briefing papers on key targets for initial approval to contact

Phase 3
(Assessment of target and price mandate)

9
Choose priority target and conduct in-depth review

10
Contact target to discover strategy-merger, JV etc If-ve response-revisit 9

11
Consider strategic fit in depth and understand specific post acquisition plan

12
Meet with target to understand key facts including price aspirations (several meetings)

13
Seek mandate to negotiate with pricing proposal, strategic fit and post acquisition policy articulated within the investment paper

Understanding
the people

6

Most acquirors considering acquisitions would expect to investigate the target's financial performance in some detail. Acquirors would also expect to understand the quality of the target's products and services relative to the marketplace. However, it is often surprising how little time is spent by acquirors investigating the management and staff of the target.

For simplicity this management investigation can be reviewed at three levels:

1 primary sources;

2 secondary sources; and

3 post site visit.

Primary sources

Directors are obliged to file a full annual return every three years with a less detailed return updating the information every year. This should at least provide the following information:

1 full name;

2 address;

3 date of birth;

4 profession;

5 other company interests; and

6 shareholdings.

As we have seen above, annual returns can be obtained either direct from Companies House itself or via a number of organisations which act as agents.

For directors of public companies additional primary sources are the annual reports which the companies themselves publish for shareholders. These are available from the companies direct, their registrars and in most cases the Financial Times Annual Reports Service. In addition to these free services, agents like Extel and Disclosure will provide annual reports for both UK and overseas quoted companies for a fee (typically £15 to £20 per company).

It can also, on occasion, be worth pursuing professional organisations for biographical information. Some professional organisations publish their own industry's 'Who's Who', while in other cases the membership department may be able to furnish limited biographical details.

Secondary sources

There are a number of directories of long standing which aim to provide information on UK company directors:

1 Directory of Directors – useful for listing directorships, but biographical and career information is very brief.

2   Who's Who in Industry – biographical and career information but self-penned, so some entries are brief.

3   Who's Who in the City – usefulness limited by coverage.

Retrospective searching of newspapers and trade journals can yield much material on senior directors of major companies. As usual a search of this kind is best accomplished by searching on-line. FT Profile is probably the most likely to yield results when information is sought on those who are neither famous nor notorious because its McCarthy file has some coverage of local newspapers.

CCN Business Information databases allow access to director information by either company name or the director's name and in addition to the basic annual return details will also provide credit data, evidence of any county court judgements and an electoral roll check.

Even a systematic and thorough trawl through all of the sources mentioned above may not produce very rich pickings. It should, however, (and in this regard the credit checking databases like CCN and Infocheck are particularly helpful) insure against any future shocks. Irregular or delinquent behaviour is almost certain to appear on their records even if it was not deemed to be newsworthy.

Post site visit

The important points mentioned above are key but there is no substitute for meeting the senior managers and shareholders to establish their objectives.

Assessing the senior managers begins at the first meeting preferably on site.

Observe their approach to this first meeting:

1   Are they well prepared?

2   Do they have a strong grasp of their business?

3   Do you recognise their comments on the sector?

4   Are they aware of their competitors?

5   Who wins the work?

6   Who really wants to leave the business?

7   Why are they selling?

Discover their achievements in the business. Question who does what within the management team. Don't believe organisation charts.

Throughout the process, acquirors must assess the true worth of the management team and their likely roles post acquisition.

Real life example – quality of management

A niche contractor in the South of England looked an attractive target for a large listed group. However, the two main directors were aged 51 and 66. Closer inspection revealed relatively inexperienced second tier management in their early 30's who had been managed autocratically by the double act at the top. This was not revealed from the comprehensive structure chart advertised in all the offices.

Conclusion

Post acquisition management difficulties were identified and material problems in managing the business were foreseen. The acquiror walked away from the deal.

Remember that as an acquiror it is important to sell the benefits of working within your group – career development, growth for the business, enhanced marketing opportunities, comprehensive management training and of course the impression that it is an enjoyable experience working within the acquiring group. The exact message to be conveyed must be specific to each vendor opportunity, credible and deliverable.

Another point worth noting is that shareholders are often going through an emotional upheaval in selling their business. Therefore clarification of the vendor's agenda at every opportunity is always helpful. Priorities can change in vendors' minds throughout the process and this should be dealt with sympathetically.

The final key message on the people agenda is to clarify, as soon as possible, the post acquisition management team. This has two immediate benefits, firstly it identifies the key vendor shareholders who are vital to the business, and secondly it establishes a management cost structure going forward.

It is now appropriate to consider in depth the post acquisition plan relevant to each target.

The Acquisition Approvals Model

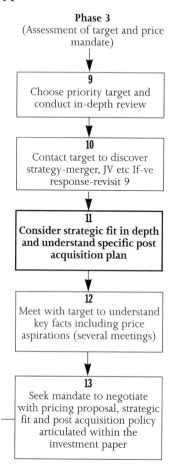

Phase 3
(Assessment of target and price
mandate)

9
Choose priority target and
conduct in-depth review

10
Contact target to discover
strategy-merger, JV etc If-ve
response-revisit 9

11
**Consider strategic fit in depth
and understand specific post
acquisition plan**

12
Meet with target to understand
key facts including price
aspirations (several meetings)

13
Seek mandate to negotiate
with pricing proposal, strategic
fit and post acquisition policy
articulated within the
investment paper

Post acquisition planning

7

As discussed earlier in this book, the key issue for any practical guide on acquisitions is how to change the odds to the acquiror's advantage.

Why do so many acquisitions fail in the eyes of acquirors? Why are so many deals badly priced and structured?

The answer lies partly in the approach taken by acquisition teams.

The Acquisition Approvals Model forces post acquisition management to the top of the agenda ahead of price and deal structure.

The model asks the question: how will the acquiror run the target business?

Only if an acquiror is comfortable with the post acquisition plan, will the target's real specific value to that acquiror be known.

Post acquisition management in its simplest form is about who will run the target in the first 12 months and how it will be integrated into the acquiring group.

The post acquisition framework which should improve the rigour of thinking will include:

1 Confirm and document deal objectives.

2 Link commercial due diligence (investigations into sector, target and management) conclusions to running the business.

3   Confirm, document, assess and prioritise business opportunities.

4   Assess management organisation structure.

5   Establish the acquisition integration management team.

6   Develop detailed integration or rationalisation plans.

Deal objectives

Deal objectives vary depending on the circumstances of each deal.

Will the acquiror be merging the target with their existing business within the sector? Is the target being kept as a stand alone operation? Perhaps the post acquisition strategy is a half-way house, allowing some partial integration to take advantage of group accounting or systems or marketing. It is common, for example in the contract catering world, to purchase businesses on the assumption that overheads of the target will be completely rationalised. The acquiror then consolidates gross margin (contracts with customers with attendant chef costs at each site) with its existing larger contracts management structure.

At the opposite end of the spectrum a specialist media company may be kept as a stand alone unit, leaving the chemistry and culture intact to allow growth to continue. Additional resources from the group may centre purely on finance and contacts.

Linking commercial due diligence to post acquisition planning

By investigating the nature of the sector in which the target operates, the detailed facts and figures of the target and the background of the management and shareholders, the acquiror will understand what is possible post acquisition.

It is the linking nature of the Acquisition Approvals Model which offers the greatest benefits to acquirors. Post acquisition planning cannot be done in a vacuum but must be based on hard evidence gathered from the investigation.

Business opportunities

The acquisition team needs to identify the strategic fit at an early stage with their group. This is not only about improvements to the target's sales line but also improvements to the acquiror's group.

Case study

An acquisitive telecoms distributor identified, at an early stage, new geographical areas overseas for expansion for the target company and new technology products to expand the sales line. However there were also profitable opportunities for the acquiror in 'farming' the target's customer base including customers that the acquiror had failed to crack themselves.

In addition to the upside, of course, all buyers must be wary of complacency. For example, it is quite common to discover major conflicts between acquiror and target's customer lists. Which customers will be lost because of the acquisition?

Management structure

Again the detailed investigation to date will have thrown up a clear picture of the target management team. Owner/managers will have made their intentions clear.

How will the acquiror manage the target business?

There are many issues to get right.

Acquirors often don't realise that ironically when you are buying you are actually 'delivering a sales message'. There is a tremendous opportunity for acquirors to win the hearts and minds of vendor management especially those not enjoying a capital gain. The following key areas should be considered:

- Clear sense of new corporate direction and strategy.
- Clear accountability and reporting structures.
- Communications plan to set out implications and advise on progress.
- Highly visible new management.
- Project plan/critical time-scales.
- Difficult and tough news broken early.
- Cultural issues planned for.
- Key players' retention.

Acquisition integration management team

The first six to twelve months post completion are vital to ensure the deal is a success.

Making things happen is the key. The best planning in the world will not succeed without dedicated managers charged with implementing the changes.

Developing integration plans

The plans need to cover the key aspects of the business.

People As discussed above, the people plan must flow from a combination of the homework done to establish the current structure and skills base and the future plan which articulates how the acquiror will run the business.

Marketing Will there be a sales force rationalisation? How can the vendor benefit from group marketing campaigns? What business opportunities exist for the vendor using buyer contacts and relationships?

How does the vendor win business? What is missing from the marketing mix?

Premises & equipment What is the current state of the asset base? Is there a need for major expenditure? Can we rationalise premises? Can we improve the capacity of existing factories using internal requirements?

Finance How is cash flow controlled? What is the cost of finance? How can the acquiror improve working capital?

Systems Are they obsolete? In the short-term can the acquiror make use of group systems to improve the target's competitiveness? Can the acquiror benefit from the quality of the vendor's system? Is compatibility a big issue?

The Acquisition Approvals Model forces acquisition teams to consider in great detail post acquisition issues, with the knowledge that has been gathered from a thorough commercial due diligence process.

Only with this approach, comprehensively executed, can acquirors turn to valuation and deal structures.

The next chapter looks at the pricing of companies from an acquiror's perspective.

The Acquisition Approvals Model

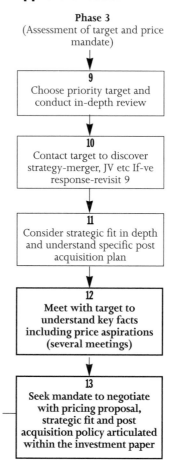

Phase 3
(Assessment of target and price mandate)

9
Choose priority target and conduct in-depth review

10
Contact target to discover strategy-merger, JV etc If-ve response-revisit 9

11
Consider strategic fit in depth and understand specific post acquisition plan

12
Meet with target to understand key facts including price aspirations (several meetings)

13
Seek mandate to negotiate with pricing proposal, strategic fit and post acquisition policy articulated within the investment paper

Valuation and pricing tips

8

The first point to make on valuation is the author's belief in the following assertion:

'Buyers perceive value: vendors aspire to price.'

It is the buyer who needs to take a personal view of value based on how the buyer will run and benefit from owning the target.

On the other hand, at the heart of a vendor's price perception is an aspiration for top dollar.

Therefore buyers need to examine the findings of the commercial due diligence and the post acquisition planning exercises very carefully before commencing the valuation exercise.

Appendix I acts as a good summary of the type of information needed prior to valuation.

It is now possible to assess value through a range of techniques as a benchmark for commencing negotiations.

Tools of the trade

The four main techniques worth noting are as follows:

1 price earnings ratios;

2 return on investment;.

3 discounted cash flows; and

4 net asset backing.

Price earnings ratios (PERs)

A listed company has a price earnings ratio noted everyday in the Financial Times. It comprises the following:

$$PER = \frac{\text{Current share price}}{\text{Earnings (profit after tax) per share}}$$

$$= \frac{\text{Market capitalisation divided by number of shares}}{\text{Earnings divided by number of shares}}$$

$$= \frac{\text{Market capitalisation}}{\text{Earnings}}$$

e.g.
PER quoted share

Share price	£5.00
Earnings	£20 million
Number of shares	40 million

$$PER = \frac{5}{20/40} = \frac{5}{0.5} = 10$$

Financial Times
Saturday 1 March 1997

FTSE Actuarial Share Indices   **The UK Series**

Produced in conjunction with the Faculty and Institute of Actuaries

	Feb 28	Day's chge%	Feb 27	Feb 26	Feb 25	Year ago	Div ytd%	Net cover	P/E ratio	Xd adj ytd	Total Return
FTSE 100	4308.3	-0.7	4339.2	4329.3	4344.7	3752.7	3.68	2.08	16.29	14.68	1808.58
FTSE 250	4654.4	-0.2	4663.0	4660.7	4665.0	4236.4	3.38	1.50	24.66	10.08	1912.0
FTSE 250 ex IT	4697.2	-0.1	4703.3	4700.1	4704.1	4256.2	3.46	1.52	23.68	9.96	1934.14
FTSE 350	2134.0	-0.6	2146.9	2142.8	2149.2	1876.0	3.62	1.97	17.55	6.71	1829.75
FTSE 350 Higher Yield	2048.4	-0.4	2056.1	2055.0	2065.8	1875.2	4.73	1.86	14.21	3.20	1479.54
FTSE 350 Lower Yield	2227.0	-0.8	2245.4	2238.1	2239.9	1881.9	2.51	2.17	22.91	10.49	1571.80
FTSE SmallCap	2353.90	-0.1	2356.22	2353.35	2352.31	2058.71	2.90	1.66	25.93	5.74	1971.60
FTSE SmallCap ex IT	2364.78	—	2365.21	2362.03	2360.19	2039.13	3.06	1.74	23.50	5.57	1995.05
FTSE All-Share	2107.86	-0.6	2119.74	2115.81	2121.62	1852.03	3.56	1.95	18.02	6.51	1834.67

FTSE Actuaries Industry Sectors

	Feb 28	Day's chge%	Feb 27	Feb 26	Feb 25	Year ago	Div ytd%	Net cover	P/E ratio	Xd adj ytd	Total Return
10 MINERAL EXTRACTION(20)	3978.42	-1.0	4016.58	4004.71	3972.24	3284.17	3.76	2.10	15.82	15.36	1750.50
12 Extraction Industries(5)	4007.05	-1.1	4051.24	4027.19	4023.19	4171.31	4.04	2.33	13.26	0.00	1194.30
15 Oil, Integrated(3)	4080.67	-0.9	4119.46	4113.02	4069.93	3327.65	3.99	2.08	15.07	20.17	1846.82
16 Oil Exploration & Prod(12)	3478.81	-0.8	3508.42	3471.01	3480.05	2247.99	1.56	1.79	44.68	0.00	2109.12
20 GEN INDUSTRIAL(272)	1993.55	-0.3	1998.90	1969.96	2000.49	2071.66	3.94	1.88	16.81	2.11	1116.59
21 Building & Construction(35)	1369.07	-0.1	1369.82	1363.20	1363.57	1105.57	3.00	1.70	24.46	1.54	1170.40
22 Building Matts & Merchs(32)	1873.53	-0.2	1877.10	1871.16	1875.32	1911.68	4.25	2.54	11.59	0.44	968.48
23 Chemicals(26)	2339.72	-0.3	2345.72	2341.74	2345.71	2533.87	4.46	1.42	19.75	0.56	1136.05
24 Diversified Industries	1448.03	-0.1	1449.93	1451.67	1460.77	1788.40	4.95	1.61	15.67	4.02	839.83
25 Electronic & Elect Equip(39)	2247.75	-0.7	2262.47	2234.82	2271.34	2364.61	3.48	1.34	26.74	1.22	1194.40
26 Engineering(70)	2546.46	-0.2	2551.72	2532.26	2546.69	2332.54	3.24	2.40	16.08	3.67	1577.88
27 Engineering, Vehicles(13)	2854.10	-0.1	2856.50	2840.72	2844.08	2645.50	3.80	1.71	19.20	0.25	1507.59
28 Paper, Pckg & Printing(27)	2513.41	-0.6	2529.63	2537.39	2543.49	2723.07	4.14	1.79	16.86	0.00	1072.12
29 Textiles & Apparel(14)	1076.35	-0.1	1077.10	1076.48	1081.05	1489.95	6.53	1.29	14.81	2.25	682.45
30 CONSUMER GOODS(85)	4093.93	-0.6	4120.47	4111.52	4128.25	3599.54	3.55	1.90	18.55	12.53	1553.19
32 Alcoholic Beverages(7)	2721.36	-1.3	2756.86	2749.48	2815.97	2800.98	4.74	1.87	14.10	31.28	1019.37
33 Food Producers(25)	2831.70	-1.0	2859.85	2862.99	2864.87	2555.89	3.84	1.80	18.10	5.07	1312.96
34 Household Goods(17)	2865.41	-1.0	2893.61	2933.37	2905.64	2538.26	3.51	2.23	15.95	1.06	1156.92
36 Health Care(16)	2259.29	-0.4	2267.27	2267.14	2281.30	1954.87	2.61	1.89	25.32	4.13	1398.50
37 Pharmaceuticals(18)	6408.50	-0.5	6438.49	6385.93	6391.15	5074.97	2.67	1.84	25.41	13.45	2219.08
38 Tobacco(2)	4488.36	…	4489.62	4556.03	4565.27	4836.87	5.78	2.13	10.18	0.00	1155.83
40 SERVICES(273)	2676.07	-0.6	2693.43	2691.23	2701.60	2337.26	2.83	1.97	22.34	7.68	1423.27
41 Distributors(30)	2741.24	-0.6	2756.91	2753.92	2768.22	2634.22	3.11	1.99	20.20	0.46	1030.75
42 Leisure & Hotels(31)	3492.77	-1.0	3527.39	3525.51	3529.23	2942.46	2.55	1.66	29.45	18.16	1910.63
43 Media(44)	4319.66	-0.7	4349.74	4342.21	4384.59	3852.01	2.21	2.12	26.73	11.48	1586.48
44 Retailers, Food(15)	1939.45	-0.9	1956.58	1942.60	1948.96	1870.32	4.08	2.31	13.27	4.28	1265.51
45 Retailers, General(53)	2111.97	-0.6	2124.25	2123.55	2132.18	1928.86	3.09	2.02	20.03	6.94	1237.86
47 Breweries, Pubs & Rest(22)	3409.69	-0.2	3416.74	3415.36	3422.50	3003.57	3.19	2.10	18.68	16.99	1681.92
48 Support Services(56)	2995.55	-1.1	3027.92	3031.41	3036.50	2121.34	1.69	2.47	29.98	1.46	1934.79
49 Transport(22)	2850.59	-0.2	2857.54	2866.78	2858.60	2320.81	3.38	1.26	29.44	6.35	1221.23
60 UTILITIES(31)	2704.29	-0.9	2729.30	2730.26	2749.13	2479.06	4.94	1.49	16.92	5.34	1229.01
62 Electricity(10)	2856.88	-0.5	2871.96	2870.41	2875.05	2795.49	5.89	2.20	9.63	22.08	1577.97
64 Gas Distribution(2)	1589.76	-3.1	1640.23	1623.41	1658.74	1601.05	7.67	*	*	0.00	869.87
66 Telecommunications(8)	2274.65	-0.8	2293.55	23 5.42	2322.86	2039.01	3.67	1.56	21.56	0.38	1074.00
68 Water(11)	2525.75	-0.6	2536.41	2516.44	2525.55	2099.73	5.89	2.31	9.18	0.00	1460.81
69 NON-FINANCIALS(681)	2153.24	-0.6	2167.21	2162.97	2169.74	1956.63	3.62	1.86	18.51	5.48	1682.75
70 FINANCIALS(106)	3920.23	-0.2	3928.82	3921.81	3928.05	2955.51	3.55	2.36	14.92	20.47	1739.44
71 Banks, Retail(8)	5724.84	-0.3	5739.58	5743.16	5748.97	4186.33	3.41	2.65	13.85	44.80	1931.21
73 Insurance(18)	1728.93	+0.1	1726.90	1699.73	1722.66	1482.37	4.88	2.15	11.91	4.50	1343.28
74 Life Assurance(7)	4574.10	-0.7	4608.12	4575.76	4583.31	3583.56	3.52	2.13	16.67	0.00	1944.75
77 Other Financial(29)	3248.06	+0.2	3241.29	3247.92	3215.77	2543.04	3.16	2.02	19.59	1.32	1899.50
79 Property(44)	1896.05	-0.1	1898.70	1900.77	1904.12	1450.59	3.37	1.33	27.98	2.57	1200.06
80 INVESTMENT TRUSTS(127)	3330.34	-0.7	3354.51	3354.66	3358.01	3134.95	2.16	1.12	51.74	8.25	1182.62
89 FTSE All-Share(914)	2107.86	-0.6	2119.74	2115.81	2121.62	1852.03	3.56	1.95	18.02	6.51	1834.67
FTSE Fledgling	1336.16	-0.2	1338.41	1337.44	1338.47	1157.05	2.90	0.55	77.83	3.28	1425.23
FTSE Fledgling ex IT	1357.96	-0.1	1359.89	1358.91	1360.46	1158.65	3.17	0.49	80.00	3.44	1450.86

The problem with quoted PERs therefore, is their dependence on share prices. General sentiment in the market can shift a company's price earnings ratio dramatically during a relatively short period as evidenced by Bodyshop's ratio which was in excess of 60 in the early 90's but stood at around 17 at the end of 1994 as the market corrected its perception of profits flowing through. Nevertheless, in acquiring unquoted companies it can be useful to note the PER of a target's quoted competitor or the sector average relating to that particular target.

Discounts of up to 50% of the quoted PER are common in unfashionable sectors whilst rarity value can generate premiums way beyond the PER of a sector as listed in the FTSE Actuaries Share Indices Table (as shown opposite).

The sector averages are calculated by taking the market capitalisation of the whole sector and dividing by the post tax profits of the whole sector. Therefore, if a sector's profits are low, as in the case of Construction, but the market believes that the sector will recover, thus keeping the share price high, then the PER will look artificially high, i.e. at a point in time the 'P', based on perception in the marketplace, is high relative to the 'E', the earnings based on the actual results. As the table shows, construction is rated at a PER of 24.46 but the average is only 18.02.

As results come through PERs correct themselves reflecting amongst other things the profits achieved.

Another useful measurement is the PERs of deals done in the target's sector over the previous 12 months. As in the FTSE table illustrated, previous deals done are another benchmark to guide acquirors in choosing a sensible multiplier or PE to apply.

Therefore, in summary, by identifying a range of relevant PERs, a suitable multiplier is established for the target and then applied to the target's sustainable post tax profits.

The next key issue using PERs is establishing a **sustainable profits** figure pertinent to the acquiror.

Set out below is an illustrative example. Firstly, the acquiror will have gathered sufficient information to restate the historical performance of the vendor, for example:

Valuation example

Commercial stationery business				
		December		
£'000	1992	1993	1994	1995
Profit before tax	**300**	**400**	**450**	**540**
Add backs				
excess directors' salaries	150	150	150	150
lease costs of second cars	20	20	20	20
bad debt – exceptional			60	
daughter's horse box/ sponsorship	25	20	30	30
overseas buying trips – Brazil	30	30	30	30
Less				
rental costs of property	(25)	(25)	(30)	(20)
stock valuation			(50)	(70)
bad debt provision				(60)
litigation provision	(20)	(20)	(30)	(40)
insurance claim		(50)	(60)	
Adjusted profits	**480**	**525**	**570**	**580**

As can be seen, the owner's benefits, which will not continue post acquisition, are added back to uncover the real wealth being generated by the business.

Equally, costs not accounted for by the vendor in the past which have flattered profits need, to be deducted to establish a more accurate picture of the vendor's track record.

However, the above is only half the picture as acquirors also need to forecast how they will run the business.

The example below illustrates the practical implications of a buyer forecasting potential profits from the vendor.

		December			
£'000	1992	1993	1994	1995	Sustainable
Adjusted profits	**480**	**525**	**570**	**580**	**550**
Adjustments by buyer					
1 accounting policies					(50)
2 higher insurance cover					(50)
3 need for qualified FD					(60)
4 cost of services to be provided by group					(25)
5 enhanced buying power – share					100
6 sales force reduction- share					100
SUSTAINABLE PROFITS					**565**
FULL TAX CHARGE 33%					**(186)**
SUSTAINABLE EARNINGS					**379**

The level of sustainable profits based on restated historical results is a judgement call and in this instance a figure of £550k is chosen. The post acquisition scenario is then laid on top of this sustainable level to arrive at a level of profits the acquiror believes represents a reliable benefit accruing from the transaction.

It is worth noting that acquirors who are not prepared to share some of the upside they bring to the party (line 5 and 6 in the example) may lose out in competitive auctions.

Therefore, under the PER basis, an acquiror establishes both a relevant PER and a sustainable profit figure to arrive at a valuation. In the above example, assuming a PER of 7, the valuation is £2.6m.

Return on investment (ROI)

This is often used by acquirors as a good 'rule of thumb' to quantify the return forecast from the target. This ratio is defined as:

$$\textbf{ROI} = \frac{\text{Adjusted pre tax profit (for the second full year of ownership)}}{\text{Total acquisition price}}$$

Two points should be borne in mind: firstly, that the profits mentioned are before charging the finance cost of the investment and, secondly the second year is used for profits to allow time for the acquisition to bed down – although it may be more relevant to use the third full year of profits if an earn out deal has been structured to cover three years.

It is difficult to set a reasonable benchmark for every acquisition, but a ratio in the range 20-25% would appear to reflect the appropriate level of risk premium in addition to the cost of capital.

In the above example the calculation would be:

	£000
Pre tax profits in year 2 say	565
Initial acquisition price	2,600

$$\textbf{ROI} = \frac{565}{2,600} = \textbf{22\%}$$

For comparative purposes with other capital projects this ratio is best kept free from the burden of cost of capital. Thus the profits to be used are prior to any funding cost of the acquisition. As an acquiror if you can access low cost finance then that must be an upside to be kept to yourself.

Discounted cash flows (DCF)

This technique uses the following formula to calculate a Discount Factor:

$$\textbf{Discount Factor} = \frac{1}{(1+i)^n}$$

where i = the discount factor (the acquiror's required rate of return)

   n = the year of the cash flow.

The discount factor is then applied to the cash flows of the target to arrive at a set of discounted cash flows. At the point where these add up to zero the target's cash flows are generating a net present value of zero and the discount rate assumed in your calculation is called the Internal Rate of Return. The example opposite illustrates a DCF technique covering a five year period as applied to acquisitions.

DCF example

Acquisition Price   £2.6 million

£000	0	1	2	3	4	5
			Years			
Cash generation pre tax		600	850	936	1000	1000
Capital expenditure		(300)	(100)	(100)	(100)	(100)
Surplus assets realised		300				
Acquisition price	(2600)					
Net cash generated	(2600)	600	750	836	900	900
Discount Factors →	1	$\frac{1}{(1+0.15)^1}$	$\frac{1}{(1+0.15)^2}$	$\frac{1}{(1+0.15)^3}$	$\frac{1}{(1+0.15)^4}$	$\frac{1}{(1+0.15)^5}$
=	1	0.870	0.756	0.657	0.571	0.497
Discounted cash flow	(2600)	522	567	549	514	448

Therefore total discounted cash flow at 15% = zero

Therefore, the acquisition which cost £2.6 million has generated, pre tax, certain cash flows over a five year period which equate to an equivalent compound annual return of 15%. This technique therefore, allows acquirors to compare a range of capital projects to determine the most attractive return. In practice, the weakness with the technique is in predicting the future cash flows of the target.

Again it is difficult to be prescriptive on a 'good' rate but a compound rate of return pre tax as illustrated of 15% would be a good benchmark.

More sophisticated versions of this technique build in probabilities to the future cash flows and termination values (to take into account cash flows to infinity). In addition the calculation can be done post tax to determine the precise discounted value of a future set of post tax cash flows. In using post tax cash flows be careful to use a post tax discount rate.

The issue of which discount rate to use depends on the purpose of the calculation.

If the acquiror wishes to determine whether an acquisition will produce an acceptable equivalent compound pre tax return, given a set of future cash flows and an assumed purchase price then the discount rate will be the rate which produces a DCF of zero.

Using the technique to produce a specific value requires the acquiror to use post tax figures and a discount rate equivalent to the cost of capital for the company.

Remember also that an acquisition may produce erratic cash flows which equates to an acceptable overall IRR although the volatility and degree of risk attaching to future cash flows may render the project unacceptable.

Net asset backing

Another important measurement that acquirors should apply is the net asset backing behind the acquisition price. Specifically, if a loss making company is being reviewed for acquisition it is not only vital to assess the net asset value at the time of the deal, but also to project forward a level of net assets at the point when losses are eliminated. By its very nature a loss making company takes time to turn round and its assets will continue to diminish in value until the loss is eliminated.

A discount of up to 50% of net assets is not uncommon when purchasing a business from the receiver. The acquiror is relieving the owner of a major problem and must allow time and resources to put the business back on an even keel.

Of course, net asset valuations are just as important with quality, profitable businesses. In particular, if an acquiror is assessing a low asset backed business, such as a sales promotion company, the acquisition price may contain a large element for goodwill, the amount by which the purchase consideration exceeds net assets.

Similarly, a high net asset value company such as a heavy engineering subsidiary of a listed group, may not warrant an acquisition valuation much higher than net assets due to the weakness of the profit stream being produced by the business.

In summary, net assets are one measurement for determining an acquiror's comfort factor within the chosen acquisition price. However, there may be specific reasons why the ultimate value to the acquiror is less than net assets, or where the value of the business to the acquiror justifies a material goodwill element.

Summary of techniques

In brief, all the four main techniques have strengths and weaknesses and some of these are summarised below:

		Strengths	Weaknesses
1	**Price earnings ratios**	market rate	no cash effect
2	**ROI**	good safe target and easy to calculate	no cash effect, broad brush
3	**DCF**	reflects effect of future cash flows	difficult in practice to calculate future cash flows
4	**Net asset backing**	determines comfort factor in worst case	may not reflect benefit to buyer

Pricing and bidding tips

Auctions

The psychology of valuing businesses in a competitive auction from a buyer's perspective deserves a special mention.

The sad example of a bidder in the engineering sector, who bid £12m for a niche player in their sector and lost the bid only to discover the final sales price of £14m was less than the £16m they could have justified, is typical of tactics that can go wrong.

Remember, in bidding scenarios, the old analogy 'you don't want the job you just want the next interview'. Take each stage at a time and give it your best shot.

As new information on the vendor is released at each bidding stage, it is important that acquirors ask themselves two key questions. Firstly, do I wish to proceed given what I know and secondly, if I do wish to proceed how does this new tranche of information affect my view on value?

Another tip to remember is that if one is submitting an offer with a range of prices then the vendor will usually take the lower number to be the relevant figure to compare with other bids. Good advice must be to stick to the best shot principle with the caveat that the price is subject to due diligence.

Pricing levels

As mentioned earlier, a central tenet of this book is that buyers perceive value and vendors aspire to price. Of course the difficult question to answer is what price is the vendor aspiring to.

Watch for the attractive price level in the vendor's mind e.g. vendors will often believe (even if it is not stated) that the offer has to start with a 5 or a 6 etc. Persuade vendors, wherever possible, to share with you their aspiration but remember the final value will be justified by the buyer not the seller.

Management buy-outs

It is worth noting these special acquirors under the subject of pricing tips – the management buy-out or buy-in team. The only logic which matters when buy-out teams are pricing their companies is affordability.

The ability to service the financial instruments used to fund the acquisition is the key driver. Of course the price arrived at under these circumstances will come down to the risk preferences of the management team and their financial backers. However at debt to equity ratios of 1:1 (the safe structure for any MBO transaction) it is unlikely that an MBO team will be able to offer as high a price as a trade player.

Board mandates

The effectiveness of an acquiror can be undermined by many factors including strong or weak guidance from the Group Board. In particular it is important that the Acquisition Team leader has some latitude in pricing the deal to allow some room for manoeuvre in the final negotiations. This is not a recipe for overpaying, but senior managers tasked with closing deals must be allowed to use their initiative within pre agreed price parameters.

The next two chapters now deal with deal structures and negotiation tactics to ensure the transaction is closed successfully.

The Acquisition Approvals Model

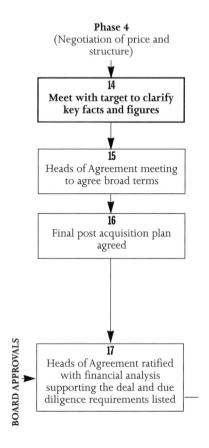

Deal structures and tax planning

9

Assets or shares

Prior to entering final negotiations ie box 14 and 15 opposite, the acquiror needs to consider the specific deal structure and tax planning issues.

There are only two ways of acquiring a business, either through the purchase of shares or the purchase of assets.

It is common for private company vendors to sell the shares of their business instead of assets because of the danger of the double tax trap. If a vendor sells assets there is a possibility of a capital gain within the company from which the assets were sold, thus crystallising a tax charge. Assuming after this event the vendor then dividends out the proceeds less tax from the disposal of the assets he is then taxed again on the receipt of the dividend. Therefore, there is a danger that through the disposal of assets a vendor is effectively taxed twice on the one transaction.

If we compare this with a vendor selling shares, the position is much simpler. The vendor exchanges shares for cash and thereby potentially creates a capital gain on those shares on which he is taxed.

From an acquiror's perspective it can be attractive to acquire assets instead of shares, because in doing so an acquiror leaves behind the history of the company in the form of hidden liabilities. In an asset purchase the acquiror identifies the assets and where appropriate the liabilities that he will be acquiring from the vendor. The purchase of specific assets would be particularly relevant in the acquisition of a business from a receiver.

However it should be noted that if the business is acquired as a going concern through an asset sale, the purchaser will be forced, under the Transfer of Undertakings (Protection of Employment) Regulations 1981 (as amended), to take on those persons who are the vendor's employees at the time of the transfer and to continue to honour the terms and conditions of employment that they enjoyed with the vendor.

Forms of purchase consideration

Although many deals are structured as a simple cash transaction at legal completion, it is possible to structure deals involving non-cash consideration to the satisfaction of all parties. Although not comprehensive, the following list illustrates the variety of purchase consideration possible:

1 Shares

2 Loanstock

3 Redeemable preference shares

4 Pre-completion dividend

5 Lump sum personal pension contribution

6 Preferential treatment of certain assets

7 Service contracts

8 Consultancy agreements

9 Restrictive covenants

In brief these items are discussed below.

Shares

Taking shares in an acquiring company can be a risky investment. However, if the proportion of shares being accepted is small relative to the overall consideration, then it may be worth taking a small risk. The advantage on the tax side is that tax is only payable when the shares are sold, and thus a gain is realised. Note: the acquiror will probably insist on managing the timing of any subsequent share sales.

From an acquiror's perspective, issuing paper, i.e. shares to vendors, is probably one of the main reasons for being listed on a stock market but depending on the terms of the deal the downside could be that the earnings per share ratio drops significantly after the deal.

Loanstock

An efficient way for vendors to receive their consideration could be by way of loanstock from the acquiror. Effectively this 'IOU' from the acquiror is redeemed by the vendor on agreed dates in the future. Assuming these are structured correctly the vendor need only pay tax when the loanstock is redeemed for cash. The key issue of course for the vendor is the security of the financial instrument, and in this regard a well informed vendor would request a bank guarantee behind the loanstock to ensure he receives payment.

Redeemable preference shares

Similarly, the vendor may receive some form of preference share with a dividend yield attaching to it, and these redeemable shares would have agreed redemption dates to suit buyer and seller. Depending on the quality of the acquiror, it may be appropriate for the vendor to consider these instruments which give him a running yield on an annual basis, but defer the tax gain until the shares are redeemed. Note: vendors run the risk with these instruments that there are insufficient reserves in the business to allow redemption.

Pre-completion dividend

Another important technique for structuring deals is the use of pre-completion dividends. The table below illustrates how these work:

Company's Books		Shareholder's Position	
	£		£
Net dividend	100	Net dividend received	100
ACT 25%	25	Tax credit 25%	25
Gross dividend	125	Gross dividend	125
		Shareholder taxed at 40%	50
		Less tax credit	(25)
		Tax due	25
		% tax rate	**25%**

Therefore, the shareholder receives, in the example above, £100 but is liable for only £25 of tax, i.e. an effective tax rate of 25%. If the vendor had received £100 by way of capital gain he may have incurred capital gains tax at 40%. (Rates may change over time.)

From an acquiror's perspective in the example above the acquiror would have to fund in the left hand side of the table the ACT of £25 until it is recoverable. Therefore, there is a cost from an acquiror's perspective and this is likely to form part of the negotiations of the final deal structure.

Lump sum pension contribution/consultancy arrangements

Items 5 to 8 on the list could be classified as deal sweeteners. They are unlikely to close material price gaps in their own right but may help to break an impasse on value.

Acquirors should understand the vendor's position on pensions and personal assets (owned by the company). It is surprising the disproportionate benefit gained by acquirors by taking a soft line on relatively minor concessions. Care should be taken to avoid financial assistance or other legal problems.

Consultancy agreements can offer solutions to buyers and sellers allowing the acquiror to access the vendor's knowledge over many years instead of a strict service contract which may not be appropriate.

Restrictive covenants

A technique not often used by acquirors is to pay some of the purchase consideration in the form of a restrictive covenant payment. If the acquiror is concerned that the vendor will commence trading in competition to the acquiror, post completion, then the restrictive covenant is applicable.

Consideration paid to the vendor for this restriction is tax allowable in the acquiror's profit and loss account subject to certain conditions.

Further deal structure tips – net asset adjustments

It is quite common for acquirors to fix their final price for the deal by reference to the value of net assets at completion. This technique allows a price to be fixed subject to the final audit of net assets. At completion a consideration is payable by the acquiror but this may be subject to additional sums being paid if audited net assets exceed the agreed amount, or, of course, if net assets are less than the agreed amount the acquiror will be due a refund of consideration. Where net asset adjustments are used it is also quite common for the use of retention accounts. The acquiror will set aside a small proportion of the consideration, probably put in Escrow with his lawyers until the net asset adjustment is completed. The Escrow account is then released to the acquiror or vendor depending on the value of the assets.

Further deal structure tips – earn-out deals

Finally on deal structures, it is worth reviewing in detail the relevance of earn-outs.

Key features

Earn-out deals are not, as one vendor once described, the purchase of a company on 'hire purchase'. They involve the purchase of 100% of the equity on day one with further consideration being payable dependant on the financial performance of future years.

From an acquiror's perspective the initial consideration will reflect profits to date of the target and take into account the current value of net assets.

The vendor is unlikely to accept an initial consideration less than net assets if the business is profitable.

In structuring earn-out deals, acquirors are likely to look for increased profit performance in future years to justify paying further tranches of acquisition consideration.

Alternatives to earn-outs

The key to any earn-out deal must be for the acquiror to keep relevant vendor management fully motivated throughout the earn-out period. This objective can be achieved by two alternative means, namely:

1   Put and call options.

2   Profit related bonus/service agreements.

Using put and call options the buyer may buy, say, 75% of the equity on day one, and negotiate with the vendor a set of call options over the remaining 25% exercisable under certain conditions. Equally a well informed vendor will negotiate the right through put options, to sell their 25% stake to the acquiror under certain conditions. Thus it is possible that a deal is structured such that the acquiror purchases 75% of the shares on day one with put and call options surrounding the remaining 25%, possibly exercisable in accordance with agreed profit targets with formulae built into the documentation to give comfort to both sides.

Alternatively, the acquiror may purchase 100% of the equity and simply put in place a large profit related bonus for the first year or two of the acquisition to ensure that vendor management are driving the business forward under new ownership.

Why use earn-out deals ?

Over the years there has been much bad press concerning the use of earn-out deals such as the fact that the vendor target company is ring-fenced from the Group for the period of the earn-out. Because of the short term hit to profits, a vendor may be reluctant to develop new markets. However, it is possible for well structured earn-out deals to allow for strategic development whilst still delivering significant capital sums to the original vendor management. These are discussed below under management control issues.

On the positive side the following reasons may justify the use of earn-outs:

1   The owners are important for future profitability.

2   The asset backing is low.

3   Profit is vulnerable e.g. through the loss of a major contract.

4   The owner is to continue as the Managing Director.

Earn-out deals may also be useful in helping to close price gaps between buyer and seller and, for some large groups divesting of non-core activities, earn-outs may be the only route for the vendor to obtain the perceived value of their non-core subsidiary.

Possible structures

Well structured deals are fit for purpose and are constructed around the desires of the vendor whilst protecting the interest of the acquiror.

Each deal structure should relate to the specific circumstances of each case. As discussed above, earn-outs may be relevant when the owner is key to the future of the business, at least in the short-term.

An earn-out formula should contain some of the following attributes:

1   A motivating multiplier of profits.

2   An average of the profits achieved during the earn-out period.

3   A hurdle performance rate below which no earn out is paid.

The rule book

The failure of earn-outs in the past may have been partly due to the lack of rigour within the legal agreements between the parties at completion. It is important that the Sale and Purchase contract contains detailed rules concerning the operation of the target company within the earn-out period. These rules would include the following:

1   Accounting policies to be used.

2   Management charges e.g. payroll, legal, treasury services.

3   Central service charges e.g. warehousing or distribution.

4   Intra group transfer pricing.

5   The cost of finance provided by the group.

6   Dividends payable to the group.

7   The appointment of auditors.

8   Rules concerning changes to staff structure.

The key to the above rules is the fact that you do not want arguments post acquisition. It may seem strange, but it may well be to the long-term advantage of an acquiror for example to provide finance to the subsidiary at a favourable rate to encourage growth strategies. This may have the effect of increasing the target's profits, and thus the earn-out consideration payable, but the business at the end of the day will have grown and the acquiring group will have achieved its objectives.

Management control issues

As an acquiror structuring earn-out deals, it is important to agree with the vendor the operational issues which will affect the success of the deal. These may include changes which alter costs e.g. a qualified finance director or an agreement on the minimum level of directors salaries as well as the maximum level. Issues surrounding non-competition with other group subsidiaries have to be discussed and documented. If business opportunities are to be pursued overseas, it may be relevant to agree separate budgets outside of the earn-out deal to encourage vendor management to pursue growth strategies. Administration issues such as budgets and monthly account preparations should be agreed between the parties as accepted requirements of the acquiror.

Acquirors must establish Board control of their vendor targets and procedures should be put in place for public announcements including dealing with customers and suppliers and any relevant legal issues affecting the company.

Above all else acquirors must remember that earn-outs do not absolve them from the responsibility of monitoring the target's business in detail, and intervening if things go wrong.

We now examine some specific tips regarding negotiation including the Heads of Agreement meeting.

The Acquisition Approvals Model

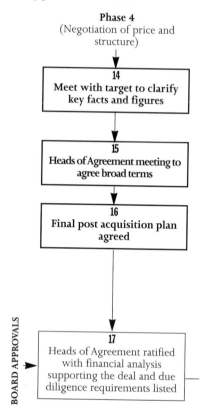

Phase 4
(Negotiation of price and
structure)

14
Meet with target to clarify
key facts and figures

15
Heads of Agreement meeting to
agree broad terms

16
Final post acquisition plan
agreed

BOARD APPROVALS

17
Heads of Agreement ratified
with financial analysis
supporting the deal and due
diligence requirements listed

Negotiation

10

Overview

It is worth noting that acquirors have the ability to spoil the final stages of the deal with poor negotiation tactics. One of the main reasons cited for acquisitions failing from an acquiror's perspective is the vendor management's attitude post the deal. It is quite likely that the attitude of vendor management has been shaped throughout the negotiation process.

Experience shows that the process is most successful when broken down into key stages. Firstly, the agreement between the parties of the major headline items and then secondly, at a later meeting, the parties should meet to negotiate a Heads of Agreement.

The headline items requiring agreement may take many meetings but will probably include the following:

1   Ball park price.

2   Assets or shares.

3   Earn-out period.

4   Assets to be excluded.

5   Directors/relatives to retire/resign.

6   Preferred purchase consideration.

7   Conditional purchase contract to defer capital gains beyond the current tax year.

8   Deadline for final negotiation.

Ball park price

It is likely that buyers and sellers will be involved in one of two types of transaction. Firstly, the auction process where the acquiror is one of many in the ring trying to acquire the target company. Special care is needed in these circumstances by acquirors. The key must be firstly to get to the next stage of the auction i.e. assuming there are various short listing stages. It would be disappointing for an acquiror to shoot low on price at an early stage in the process and be excluded from further rounds of negotiation only to find the final negotiated price is lower than they would have offered. On the other hand, if an acquiror has offered the maximum price it is prepared to pay to own the business, and its offer is still rejected, then it should be comfortable with its tactics. As always the price is a matter of judgement based on the specific circumstances of the acquiror.

If the acquiror is on a one-to-one basis with the vendor outside of an auction process, then the negotiation tactics may be different. Again, it is open to acquirors to offer their maximum price but this may not be necessary. Because vendors aspire to a price and acquirors perceive a value, the question requiring an answer is: what is the vendor's aspiration on price? (which may be less than the acquiror's perceived value).

Assets or shares

Acquirors should understand vendors' tax positions and vice versa. In most cases the issue of whether assets or shares are being sold is not a problem. However, it is important for both sides to understand the true post tax effect of both routes, assets or shares, from both a buyer's and seller's perspective. It is possible that the acquiror may have to purchase shares of the main business and assets used in the business but owned by an associate company of the target.

Earn-out period

It is recommended that earn-out deals cover no more than two years because of the need to separately legislate for operational management of the target during the earn-out. If properly documented, it is possible to allow vendor management to develop their business during the life of the earn-out as discussed earlier. However, there is a danger that beyond two years market factors may come into play which could not have been foreseen at the time of the original deal and, therefore, these factors e.g. legislation, render the 'rule book' (conditions of the sale and purchase contract) unworkable.

Assets to be excluded

This may be relevant where the acquiror may not wish to purchase property or assets owned by the target company.

The key is to establish market value as part of the negotiations, and an independent arbitrator may be useful to limit the emotional element of the discussions. It is reasonable for acquirors to regard assets, received by vendors, at discounts from market value, as part of the purchase consideration.

It is quite likely that concessions of this nature by acquirors, i.e. allowing specific assets to be sold back to vendors, will bring advantages to the acquiror way beyond the apparent value of the concession. Again care must be taken to ensure that financial assistance provisions are not triggered.

Directors/relatives to resign

It is worth stating the obvious when dealing with this delicate subject. It is quite common for private companies to employ family members in various managerial positions within the business. These people may not be fulfilling a necessary function, but this should be assessed not assumed.

Preferred purchase consideration

Well advised vendors are unlikely to take the majority of the purchase consideration in shares, even if the shares are in the most blue chip of acquirors. On the other hand well structured deals can turn an unattractive deal – pre-tax from a vendor's viewpoint – into an acceptable post-tax deal.

In terms of negotiation, don't allow preferred types of consideration to be left off the agenda until the final stages. Non-cash considerations offered by acquirors should be discussed with vendors early in the process.

Conditional purchase contract

In terms of good tax planning it may be possible to defer the capital gain on the transaction beyond the end of the tax year. For example, the vendor may agree to sell his business assuming a key tender is won, the tender success being an event likely to happen beyond the tax year.

Deadline for final negotiation

Throughout the initial negotiation meetings, it is important to maintain momentum between the parties and, although an obvious point, an effective method is to focus on a legal completion deadline as a target.

Heads of agreement

Assuming the parties have established sufficient common ground for a final negotiating meeting, it is likely to be productive for both buyer and seller to meet for one final meeting to attempt to agree the Heads of Agreement.

This meeting is so important to the final outcome of the deal that it is worth considering in some detail the agenda which both sides wish to cover. From an acquiror's perspective the following list probably covers the main issues, but the order of events must be down to judgement on the day. These may comprise:

1 **Update since last meeting**
   It is vital to clarify even at this late stage any change of information which affects the deal.

2 **Confirmation of what is included**
   It is possible that misunderstandings still exist – what are the key assets to be included in the deal?

3 **Price of certain assets to be purchased by directors**
   This is a sensitive but necessary part of the negotiation process, and must form part of the acquisition price.

4 Earn-out formula and period

Too often in deals, due to time pressure or other reasons, earn-out deals are not clarified in sufficient detail. It is important to illustrate the earn-out formula with examples to ensure all parties understand the deal.

5 Transfer of pension funds

An area often underestimated in terms of complexity. Sufficient time is required to resolve the issues. At this stage it is quite acceptable for the detailed administration of pension fund benefits to be transferred and finalised over a 6-12 month period post completion.

6 Intellectual property rights

Acquirors must ensure that the relevant rights are within the target company they are purchasing, and that they do not rest with individual directors or other companies outside of the target group.

7 Removal of personal guarantees

Acquirors will have to offer the release of guarantees which are regarded quite rightly as an important benefit by the vendors.

8 Key warranties and indemnities

Although an issue to be discussed in detail at the contract stage, it is still important that the parties involved in the deal discuss the main warranties and indemnities expected.

9 Purchase price and consideration

The final price negotiations must be agreed at this meeting and its position on the agenda should be driven by the acquiror.

10 **Exclusivity arrangements**

As an acquiror you want to establish an exclusivity or lock-out period to allow due diligence to take place without a competitive threat. Normally 8 weeks is an acceptable exclusivity period to completion.

11 **Timetable to completion**

Again, an experienced acquiror will ensure the momentum is maintained between the parties by setting future deadlines.

Final stages – pre due diligence

It is worth ensuring from the acquiror's perspective that the Group Board are happy with the final Heads of Agreement. A review at this stage of all areas of investigation and a confirmation that the post acquisition strategy is still relevant is also helpful.

The Acquisition Team leader can then seek ratification from the Group Board of the Heads of Agreement, the strategy for integration and the due diligence areas to be investigated prior to contracts.

Thus the acquiror now enters phase 5 of the Acquisition Approvals Model – due diligence and contracts. These issues are now dealt with in the final chapters to Part 1 of the book.

The Acquisition Approvals Model

Phase 5
(Legal completion)

18
Due diligence-technical
financial and operational

19
due diligence-legal

20
Contracts stage negotiation and
drafting meetings

21
Public announcements agreed

22
Post acquisition management,
30, 60, 90 day plan signed off

23
LEGAL COMPLETION

Due diligence and contracts

11

Due diligence

An acquiror now has the opportunity with the help of his advisors to conduct a detailed investigation on site.

It is important to focus the limited time available towards the key issues which underpin the strategy behind the deal, the price proposed and the deal structure negotiated.

Appendix III contains a list of accounting due diligence items to assist acquirors in briefing their investigation teams.

A few tips – if external accountants are to be used – ensure a deliverable timetable is agreed and ensure that you are happy with the track record of the personnel who will do the work. Of course, fees should be fixed and agreed in advance. Carve outs by advisors on professional indemnity issues are always an interesting area of discussion between client and advisor.

Due diligence offers acquirors the opportunity to verify the post acquisition plan.

A combination of external accountants focusing on the historical facts and figures and the internal acquisition team focusing on the post acquisition plan areas – people, marketing, premises, forecasts and systems – is often the most effective way to investigate the target.

Equally at this stage your lawyers should be seeking answers to detailed questions regarding leases, intellectual property, planning rights, capital structure etc.

The result of all this work will be a formal due diligence report by your external accountants in response to your brief. In addition your lawyers may indicate at this stage areas of concern regarding key documents.

It is important to distil down all the information from the due diligence and ask some key questions:

1   Is this vendor company strategically the business we thought we were buying?

2   Is it ex-growth and requiring some fundamental investment or re-engineering?

3   Are we now aware of material downsides that affect our view of value?

A formal review of all the facts is required and if necessary a meeting with the vendor to revisit the price and deal structure agreed.

It is important for acquirors to be both quite clear on their reasons for revisiting price and on the risks involved of the vendor terminating discussions at this stage.

Assuming a successful due diligence process the acquisition team will then brief their lawyers to issue the sale and purchase contract.

Sale and purchase contracts – non-lawyer tips

The following guidelines are aimed at helping the principals of both sides understand some of the key issues to be dealt with within the sale and purchase contract.

In some ways all points raised in a transaction are commercial ones rather than legal. In other words it is unacceptable for principals to abdicate responsibility to their lawyers for the final sale and purchase contract.

A transaction is not complete until contracts are signed. Understanding and following through the commercial agreement, embodied in the Heads of Agreement, to the final draft of the contract is a necessary evil of doing deals.

Warranties and indemnities

The purpose of both warranties and indemnities is to force the vendor to disclose key facts which may affect the acquiror's view of the business. The balance for each side's legal team is: from the acquiror's perspective, to extract sensible and comprehensive warranties and indemnities; whilst the vendor's team will attempt to resist this, and where granted, to make sufficient disclosures to render some of the warranties ineffective.

The primary difference between warranties and indemnities is that indemnities are more onerous for vendors to give, allowing the acquiror £1 for £1 compensation if an indemnity is breached. The most common indemnity granted by vendors concerns tax. A warranty given by a vendor is also valuable from an acquiror's perspective. However to obtain compensation an acquiror has to prove that a 'loss of bargain' has been incurred due to the vendor breaching the warranty. Proving a warranty breach and quantifying the subsequent loss through the courts can be

109

both time consuming and expensive as the recent Brent Walker and Grand Metropolitan legal case demonstrated.

De maximus and de minimus limits

To avoid unreasonable claims being made under the contract, both a minimum financial level (de minimus) and a maximum level (de maximus) for warranty claims is often set.

The minimum limit is usually set around £2k to £5k depending on the size of the deal. This avoids dozens of claims of small value being served by the acquiror on the vendor. Equally, the vendor usually expects the protection of a maximum financial level for claims set at the proceeds received for the business.

Earn-outs

Often, where a complicated earn-out formula is used in a transaction, there is a lack of clarity at the Heads of Agreement stage. Don't fall into this trap. Ensure both the Heads of Agreement and the Sale and Purchase Contract have appended to them worked examples of the formula used, including various assumptions on profits achieved.

Legal team

Finally, the involvement of your lawyers in a transaction at the latest possible moment may, on the face of it, keep your costs down. However this is both commercially and financially flawed.

Brief your lawyers prior to entering the Heads of Agreement meeting and after the meeting, if successful, brief them in detail on the terms of the deal and the strategic objective behind the transaction.

It is an acquiror's choice who should form part of the commercial negotiation team to agree a Heads of Agreement but in the author's experience the number of points agreed seems to vary in inverse proportion to the number of people in the room!

There should be, if at all possible, a seamless join as your lawyers merge into the acquisition team to ensure that the momentum of the deal is maintained.

The Acquisition Approvals Model

Phase 5
(Legal completion)

18	Due diligence-technical financial and operational
19	Due diligence-legal
20	Contracts stage negotiation and drafting meetings
21	Public announcements agreed
22	Post acquisition management, 30, 60, 90 day plan signed off
23	LEGAL COMPLETION

Overseas acquisitions

12

The Acquisition Approvals Model has been described in some detail from strategic visions at the beginning of the process through to legal completion and post completion reviews of lessons learned. The aim of the model is to minimise the risk of doing the wrong deal and to avoid omitting key facts from the investigation.

If these issues are important for acquirors when contemplating a transaction in their own country, then their importance must intensify when acquirors are considering an overseas acquisition.

The model will force post acquisition issues to the top of the agenda, i.e. who will run the target company post completion and how will it be integrated into the group?

Specifically with an overseas acquisition the following areas need special attention:

1 Where are the most attractive regions?

2 How will you search for the relevant targets?

3 How will you gather the relevant facts on the target?

4 How will you deal with the specific legal and tax issues in the target country?

Selecting regions

The strategic direction of the group will be reviewed as a matter of course in most well run private and public companies. This should always encompass the desirability of overseas expansion. The attractiveness of any region will vary from sector to sector.

In the food sector, barriers to entry (trade tariffs etc) are coming down every year. New dynamic geographic regions are looking increasingly attractive from the UK, e.g. Russia, China and Japan.

In the telecommunications sector, a distributor relying on the UK market may struggle to survive. Increasingly in most sectors the opportunities lie outside of the country of origin.

However, the risks of failure are far higher when contemplating an acquisition in an overseas market compared with, say, negotiating a distribution agreement.

The attractiveness of a region with reference to acquisitions may depend on:

1 The need for the local target to maintain a local shareholder base.

2 The macro-economic history of the region.

3 The political track record of the region.

4 The number of attractive targets.

5 The quality and skills base of the indigenous workforce.

6 The ability to access markets important to the existing customer base.

There is no substitute for trading in a region and working with local partners to understand the dynamics of the sector in that particular country.

In the final analysis acquiring a target in a specific overseas country will come down to your belief that the acquisition will deliver post acquisition results as planned within the specific trading environment in that country.

Acquisition search in a country

Ultimately the quality of the search will depend on the filing requirements in that country. Although the regulatory environment and accounting rules vary widely within Europe it is usually possible to obtain reasonably accurate and reliable information on companies in the major Western European economies. However developing regions like Africa and Latin America and even the so called tiger economies of the Pacific Rim do not possess this level of quality information.

In those countries where data is thin on the ground specialist help may be required. Good sources of company information and market information may include:

1   **Information centres**

- The DTI's Export Market Information Centre (EMIC) in London.

- Embassies – commercial section, chambers of commerce & industry.

2   **Tertiary sources** (guides to research sources)

- Armstrong & Fenton: World Databases in Company Information published by Bowker Saur (lists directories of company information, products, people, organisations).

- Directory of Periodicals On-line – published by Globe & Mail (Canadian Newspaper). If you were looking for business papers in Malaysia it could tell you that e.g. Malaysian

Business is bi-weekly, and published by Berita Publishing, and that Business Times of Kuala Lumpur is a daily, and that both are available on Textline.

- London Business School: Guide to European Market Information.

- European Business Information Sourcebook – published annually by Headland Business Information in conjunction with Bowker Saur.

- Sarah Ball: Directory of International Sources of Business Information (names information providers, country data, industry sources on-line).

- Headland – On-line/CD Rom Business Sourcebook.

- Directories in Print (US bias but international in scope, appears annually) edited by Dawn Couzett Des Jardins.

- Benn's Media Directory: International volume – periodicals.

- International Organisations – encyclopaedia of associations. Published by Gale edited by Theresa MacFarlane.

- CBD: Directory of European Industrial & Trade Associations. (Also UK trade associations may have overseas affiliates).

- Keynote: The Guide – practical handbook of marketing research sources in UK and W. Europe.

- Euromonitor:

  European Directory of Trade & Business Associations.

  European Directory of Marketing Information Sources.

  World Directory of Trade & Business Journals.

  World Directory of Trade & Business Information Libraries.

World Directory of Trade & Non-Official Statistical
Sources.

3 Market research

- Guides

  MarketSearch, MSI, Findex, etc.

  Euromonitor: European Directory of Consumer
  Market Reports & Surveys.

- Publishers

  Euromonitor, ICC Keynote, Mintel and EIU all follow
  overseas markets. Consumer markets best served.
  Frost & Sullivan for US industrial sectors.

4 Economic statistics

- OECD, EIU, IMF.

5 Press

- Economist, FT, etc, for surveys.

- News databases – Textline, Nexis, FT Profile, IAC databases,
  Business & Industry.

6 Classified company directory

- D&B and Kompass for worldwide coverage. Specialist local
  companies e.g. Hoppenstedt & Creditreform in Germany, ORT
  in France, etc. US and Europe best coverage.

- National directories for specific trades difficult to access even
  from EMIC.

Legal and tax issues

The key, of course, to quality overseas acquisitions is to work with strong technical people who live in the country concerned. Most large legal practices in the UK have overseas offices or affiliates who will understand the issues.

Joint ventures, strategic alliances, majority stakes or even minority stakes may be all that is possible in the preferred territory. Beware when investing in less than 100% of the equity, always ensure you sort out the 'divorce settlement' prior to marrying the target. What rights attach to the minority stake held by the State or the investment partner? Attempting to sue in an overseas court at a later date to correct an agreement can be counter-productive.

The text now concentrates on the Disposals Model to explain how attractive divestments are achieved.

part two
disposals

The Covert Controlled Auction Model

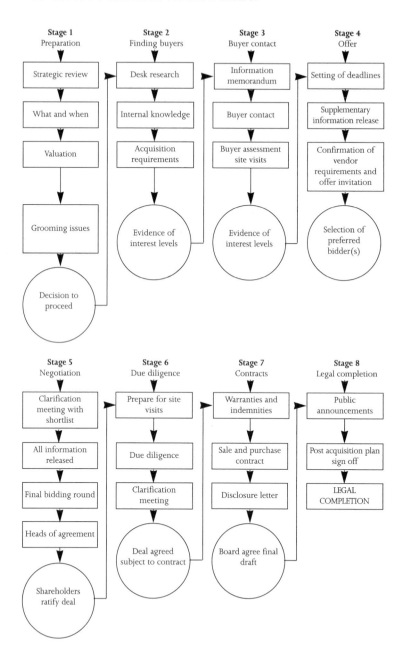

The covert controlled auction model

13

Introduction

What is the best way to sell a company? The model opposite describes an effective technique to ensure that all the issues have been considered.

Preparing for a disposal can make a material difference to the price achieved.

Unlike the acquiror's approach to the transaction, a vendor wants several parties in the ring to ensure an auction is created.

Despite the concerns of many vendors it is possible to stage-manage a covert controlled auction ensuring that only key parties are aware of the transaction until the public announcements are made.

The model breaks down into eight key phases of activity for the vendor and his advisors. The model forces the vendor to consider, at each phase, whether he is comfortable moving to the next stage.

The early stages of the model force vendors to consider alternatives to sale. Often in a family controlled business the strategic option of selling the business is dominated by the lifestyle choices available to the shareholders.

The question that should be asked by the shareholders before contemplating a sale is: what do we want to achieve with the rest of our lives? Unless private company shareholders are asking themselves fundamental questions of how they wish to run their lives then there is a danger that they are not confronting the issues. Equally, business plans and sector trends may be forcing management teams to consider their future options very carefully.

The agenda for chief executives of large listed groups is likely to be a less personal agenda and should be driven by strategic options available to the Group Board.

By forcing strategic thinking to the top of the agenda the model allows careful consideration of the options available to any vendor management team, private or listed, including financial implications.

The first stage of the model is the preparation stage.

Stage 1 – The preparation stage

A strategic review of all the options open to the vendor group is an essential first stage. The alternatives are discussed in the next chapter but include: float, management buy-out or buy-in, trade sale, selling equity to a financial institution, selling a minority stake to a larger trade player, merger using shares, a reverse into a listed shell and buying in of some of the shares.

In particular with the trade sale route the vendor will wish to understand what and when to sell: e.g. are properties, licences and name transferring with the sale?

The issue of value should also be addressed at this stage. Surely it is sensible to take an early view as a vendor shareholder body on how much the business may be worth or more importantly an agreed minimum acceptable price.

A decision can now be made on the best way forward and assuming a trade sale or strategic alliance is being considered then the next stage – finding buyers becomes relevant.

Stage 2 – Finding buyers

The ability to find potentially relevant buyers around the world for a vendor business has never been easier, the caveat is that you need the electronic databases and networks to be able to research the most relevant targets.

The key is to identify the buyer with most to gain from the deal.

In addition, attention to detail, breadth of thinking and quality of knowledge of the targets can all make a significant difference to the buyers ultimately brought into the ring and, therefore, the prices offered for the business.

Stage 3 – Buyer contact

Assuming the vendor and its advisors are comfortable with the potential appetite from the buyer population then the decision to proceed is taken.

Note: buyers at this stage should be totally oblivious to the possibility that the company or division is for sale.

This buyer contact stage comprises a grooming exercise by the vendor and the preparation of a succinct Information Memorandum.

Only when the vendor feels comfortable that the preparation is complete should the buyers be contacted.

The result of this formal contact, explaining the investment opportunity to the buyer, should be a series of meetings (assuming stage 2 has been thoroughly done) between buyer and seller. At these meetings the Information Memorandum will be discussed, further questions answered and strategic fit reviewed and explored.

At the end of this stage the vendor will assess whether success is likely with any of the parties in the ring. Again assuming there is strong interest, the vendor may choose to invite offers at this early stage to reduce the number of parties involved.

Alternatively, if only a few parties have been invited into the ring, then the vendor should proceed according to a formal timetable to offers.

Stage 4 – Offer

This is an important stage which allows the vendor to ensure that the buyer has sufficient information to deliver a full offer.

The exact nature of the supplementary information will vary from deal to deal but should be standardised within each deal to ensure all buyers are on a level playing field.

An aggressive timetable will force potentially attractive purchasers out of the bidding and may give the impression of undue haste or even the impression of a distressed sale. On the other hand the momentum of the deal should be maintained.

Vendors need to make clear exactly what they require from the buyer within the offer document – including price, extent of due diligence, conditions of the offer and post acquisition strategy.

Offers should therefore be received and a decision made by the vendor whether to proceed with any of the parties. It may make sense at this stage to shortlist two or more attractive parties to clarify the details of their offer.

Stage 5 – Negotiation

Whether there is a need to hold several clarification meetings and invite a final round of bidding is a matter of judgement.

The important decision to be made is which party is to be given preferred bidder status.

This party will be invited to a final negotiation meeting to clarify the terms of the deal – the Heads of Agreement meeting.

This meeting was discussed in some detail in chapter 10. However the meeting is discussed in Chapter 17 from a vendor's perspective.

Assuming a successful meeting, both Boards should then ratify the deal before proceeding to due diligence.

Stage 6 – Due diligence

Vendors need to manage this due diligence process. Remember the vendor has not sold the business yet!

Access to the books of account needs to be controlled and site visits kept to a minimum. Chapter 18 offers some tips for vendors to ensure this stage is done efficiently.

Especially where an earn-out structure is envisaged, vendors should also use this stage to verify some key facts and figures about the buyer – including previous track record in managing acquisitions.

Stage 7 – Contracts

Finally a sale and purchase contract will be issued by the acquiror, unless the vendor has taken the initiative and produced a first draft for discussion.

At Chapter 18 a range of tips is offered to vendors to assist them in understanding some of the issues to expect in the sale and purchase contract.

Another important area for vendors is the Disclosure Letter. Time should be taken over the details of this document by all vendor shareholders, reviewing relevant areas of the business with their lawyers.

Finally the completed version of the contract will be ratified by both Boards and a formal signing session is then arranged.

Stage 8 – Legal completion

The ability of both sets of lawyers in a transaction to turn the legal completion meeting into an all night sitting of the debating society never ceases to amaze even experienced observers. However, often important documents are produced at the last minute leaving the lawyers struggling to complete the drafting at the pre-arranged time.

Agreeing public announcements is also an important issue to deal with at this stage. Both buyer and vendor will wish to get their message across to staff within the wording of the document.

Both parties should take the opportunity to emphasise the positive aspects of the deal and the opportunities to be grasped in the coming months.

These stages are now examined in detail starting with the preparation stage.

The Covert Controlled Auction Model

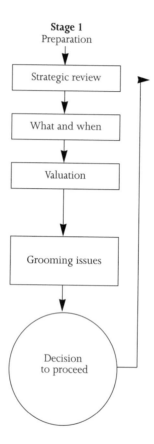

The preparation stage

14

This stage includes a strtegic review, what and when to sell, grooming issues and how much the business is worth.

Vendors need to consider carefully all aspects of their business, its competitive position and the strategic options available to it prior to contemplating a disposal.

They will find a formal strategic review invaluable in helping them decide the best way forward.

The strategic review

The options discussed below are focused towards the family company but the main ones are also relevant to non-core subsidiaries of listed groups.

Often in private companies the owners of the business are at a 'T' junction. Doing nothing is not an attractive option. Selling the business may be the correct option but the main driver for the vendors is the need for change due to many factors, such as: boredom, competitive edge being eroded, the need for a major investment in equipment, illness, acquisition opportunities becoming available or a large minority shareholder wanting to leave the business.

Whatever the reason for change it must be helpful to understand the strategic options open to the vendor.

This review should compare the following options:

1 Flotation

2 Selling a minority stake to a venture capitalist

3 Selling a minority stake to an industrial partner

4 Merging the business using paper

5 Recapitalising the group to acquire relevant targets

6 Selling a majority or entire shareholding to a third party.

Flotation

A flotation is not an exit for shareholders who manage the business. The rule of thumb is that investing institutions will expect vendor management to retain around 75% of their holdings.

Can you float the business? Ideally a business should be generating at least £3 million pre tax profits. This should place a minimum market capitalisation of between £25 to £30 million on the entity. Below this level there is a worry that the business will not attract the attention of sufficient investors and therefore the liquidity of the shares will be limited.

Continuing obligations of the business need to be considered. Does the management understand the Cadbury and Greenbury recommendations?

Are the strategic plans robust and do they demonstrate strong compound growth?

Has the management team considered the six month treadmill of the results announcements? Has the management assessed the time required to deal with City issues?

There are many issues to be considered in assessing flotation but the important point is to objectively compare the deliverability of the float, the cost and the advantages and disadvantages against the objectives of the shareholders and the strategic requirements of the business.

Selling a minority stake to a venture capitalist

Bringing a venture capitalist onto the shareholder register can allow vendor shareholders to crystallise some of their paper wealth without losing control. It can allow a significant war chest to be raised for acquisition or capital expenditure on plant. It can also allow a significant minority shareholder to retire with a reasonable reward. In many instances it has improved the profile of the investee company and repaired a damaged balance sheet in the process.

The downside: the investing institution is probably looking for a fixed dividend, a profit dividend, a return on exit equivalent to a compound annual return in excess of 30% and a seat on the Board.

Selling a minority stake to an industrial partner

It is possible to sell a minority stake to an industrial partner to accelerate the growth of a business. The vendor business may be a niche technology or software house requiring an alliance to develop products quickly enough for the fast changing marketplace.

In this scenario, the bigger brother gets access to specialist technology at an early stage in its development. The phrase 'corporate venturing' is sometimes used to describe early stage businesses which go down this route. For a more mature private company it may be a route to a profitable trading relationship especially when the larger partner can open doors into overseas markets or new industrial sectors.

A tip mentioned earlier in the book regarding joint ventures is to ensure the agreement allows you to part company with your new minority partner if things don't work out. Alternatively, the vendor shareholders should put in place an option agreement to sell their remaining shares at a later date at an attractive multiple of profits.

Merging the business using paper

The theory of merging two private companies in a share swap arrangement to create a stronger, better focused, more efficient new group sounds attractive. The difficulty of this proposal is delivering the solution.

Persuading two private company chairmen of the relative value of each other's private company shares and the merits of who should be the new chief executive of the enlarged group is not easy!

However in certain circumstances it may be possible to merge two businesses together to satisfy the objectives of both shareholding companies. External finance may need to be raised in the process to allow some shareholders to exit.

Recapitalising the group to acquire relevant targets

Ironically, the management team may wish to consider, as one of their strategic options, growing the business by acquisition – ie. instead of looking at exit strategies perhaps a growth strategy involving acquisition is required.

It is possible to restructure the target company using external finance, allow some shareholders to exit and complete a significant acquisition contemporaneously.

The danger for most private companies is that they are not ready for an acquisition and underestimate the resources and skills required to plan and execute them successfully.

Selling a majority or entire shareholding to a third party

The remainder of this book illustrates in detail how to sell a business. However, within the context of a strategic review the following points are relevant:

1   Does the profit stream indicate a subsidiary that is ex-growth?

2   Who are obvious purchasers of the business?

3   What are the likely values achievable from a trade sale?

4   Are there weaknesses in the management team and is this important to an acquiror?

5   What is happening in the sector to suggest that the vendor may have rarity value or, conversely, be unsaleable?

The strategic review therefore should spell out: the options; the possible proceeds to shareholders resulting from the options; the deliverability of them; and, as a by-product, improvements needed to the business.

Preparation, post strategic review

Assuming the trade sale route is the preferred option going forward, there are four specific aspects that need to be addressed from a vendor's perspective:

* What to sell?

* When to sell?

* Improvements needed/grooming tips

* How much is the business worth?

These are now addressed in detail.

What to sell?

Firstly, vendors should decide whether to sell assets or shares. The issues involved are discussed in Chapter 17.

If the business being sold is the major company within the group, the vendor will probably wish to sell either the group holding company shares or sell the vendor company subsidiary shares. However a large private group selling a non-core subsidiary may welcome the opportunity to sell assets and create capital gains within the group structure.

Property is an area worth considering separately. If the business enjoys the use of a property, owned separately by the vendors outside of the balance sheet, then a decision is needed as to whether it should be sold with the business. Does the vendor wish to receive rental income from the property after the business is sold?

Private assets, boats, planes, second, third, or fourth cars, overseas villas or sales offices need to be addressed. Is the balance sheet clean of private assets? If not then a grooming exercise has to be addressed or at least a strategy planned to deal with it.

Is the name of the company going across with the business? This is more of an issue in a group holding structure where the non-core subsidiary may trade under a group name. Hunting and Thorn have both sold businesses over the years where the subsidiary had to lose its name for that reason.

When to sell?

Estate agents had rarity value in 1988 and were unsaleable in 1992. Niche printing businesses, specialist tool hire companies, branded food businesses and niche publishing businesses have all attracted premium prices in the 1990's because, amongst other reasons, they possessed **rarity** value at the time.

There is no right time to sell. The private company shareholders that rejected an offer of £5 million for their business in 1989 but accepted £2 million in 1995 may have been a little frustrated but surprisingly did not regret the original decision. They made that decision based on the facts as they saw them at the time. Unfortunately circumstances change.

The sobering fact is that a vendor can raise profits say 20% over a two year period but be worth less at the end of that period than at the beginning because **sentiment** has gone against the sector e.g. mechanical and electrical contracting in the early 1990's. As explained in Chapter 8 the Price Earnings Ratio or the Multiple of Profits used to value a private company is just as important as the underlying profits.

Equally, the vendor with an impeccable track record of rising profits may wait too long. If **profits suffer** a small dip then this can cause cynical buyers to discount the value of the business disproportionately to the drop in profits.

In terms of the **statutory accounts**, ideally, a vendor should have an up-to-date set of audited accounts and be talking to buyers when the current forecasts are impressive and deliverable.

The **sector** itself may be undergoing dramatic changes which require careful monitoring regarding the timing of a sale.

A good example of this is the speed of change in the bus sector. Acquirors have moved so quickly to mop up the smaller independents in the sector that many large acquirors now face OFT problems if they attempt to acquire in certain regions. Independents in the sector may find themselves unsaleable to attractive buyers due to regulatory constraints.

The business plan may indicate key drivers to be at all time highs. Advertisement revenue driven magazines in the mid 1980's secured premium prices prior to the advertising collapse in late 1988.

Finally, with respect to timing, vendors should realise that if they are managing a low asset backed, profitable service company then the deal structure will probably involve an **earn-out** (payment of consideration based on future performance). In these instances a vendor wishing to exit from a business on disposal may have to wait three years post completion before the final tranche of consideration is paid.

Valuation and pricing tips

Valuation

One of the central tenets of this book is that acquirors perceive value and vendors aspire to price. However, vendors, with the help of their advisors, should review possible values for the business.

Chapter 8 Valuation and pricing tips explains the main 'tools of the trade' and how they are applied by measured acquirors.

The importance of the vendor shareholders reviewing value at this preparation stage is not to put a price on the business for the benefit of outsiders. It is to establish two facts. Firstly, that the shareholders have similar aspirations on price and, secondly, that the vendor's advisor believes the price is deliverable. If either of these facts cannot be established a re-think is required. Divisions in the vendor team will be exploited at the later stages of the Covert Controlled Auction Model by an experienced purchaser.

Grooming tips

In this preparation stage vendors should be aware of some grooming tips which should help underpin value and therefore maximise price.

Firstly, **one off costs** incurred by the business should be documented and will be added back to profits in later presentations to buyers. Annual conference costs which had to be spent by the marketing department to underpin the brand are not acceptable add-backs! However, bad debts of a material and unusual nature or one off litigation costs are probably acceptable.

The **Statutory Books** should be brought up to date to give the correct impression and to ensure all paperwork is filed as required.

This may be a good time to tidy up the **shareholder register** by buying in some small minority shareholders. Remember an acquiror needs 90% of the equity before he can compulsorily purchase the remaining 10%. Vendors do not want an 11% minority shareholder spoiling an attractive deal, for whatever reason.

A well prepared and timely set of **management accounts** is always a good sign for a buyer. The ability to explain the movements of the main volume and yield drivers within the business as well as the financial performance is always impressive. Remember there are only two reasons behind the movement of a gross profit revenue or cost item: volume and yield.

Are **employment contracts** up to date and well documented, especially for the senior management team?

Planning consents should be reviewed to ensure they are comprehensive and transferable. Necessary changes to these can be time consuming and without them a buyer may not be able to proceed.

Pensions can cause massive problems if paperwork has not been kept up to date. Has an actuarial valuation been completed in the recent past?

137

Accounting policies should be reviewed for reasonableness especially relative to competitors in the sector. Is the vendor flattering to deceive?

Are **tax computations** signed off and up to date or has the vendor an ongoing problem with the local inspector? Problems of this nature can act as a poison pill to buyers.

Finally, is the **management team** complete? Are there weaknesses which should be addressed whether the business is sold or not.

The above set of tips can be crystallised in a light hearted list of key attributes that all vendors can review, **The Vendor saleability test.**

Vendor saleability test

What are potential buyers looking for in a business?

Answers are given on a scale of 0 to 5, 5 denoting strong agreement and 0 denoting stong disagreement.

Company has a stong market position in its sector ☐
High quality second-tier management ☐
Vendor has strong desire to stay ☐
Business does not need to be sold to survive? ☐
Business not dependent on major customer
(more than 30% of sales with one cutomer = 0) ☐
Individual sales orders represent less than 10% of sales ☐
Statutory accounts up to date ☐
Company has grown consistently in past 3 years ☐
Current year trading and forecasts ahead of previous year ☐
Strong order book (more than 12 months = 5) ☐
Strong pre-tax profit? ☐
Vendor free from non-core activities ☐
Simple share structure ☐
Accounting policies in line with sector ☐
Pre-tax profit/sales margin above sector average ☐
TOTAL ☐

A score of 60 or above implies you own a highly saleable business, probably at a peak in valuation terms. A score below 60 but above 46 implies a quality business with a few grooming issues worth addressing. A score below 46 but above 30 implies a good business but which contains problems that need to be addressed to ensure the maximum proceeds are realised from a sale. A score of 30 or below implies a business that needs to address some fundamental issues to ensure that shareholder value is not eroded in the short to medium term. A business in this category is probably not saleable at the present time.

A health warning to note is that the test is designed to highlight possible deficiencies in saleability. Selling a private company is not a science but attention to key grooming issues over time can make a material difference to the value obtained for private company shareholders whatever exit route is chosen.

We have discussed in detail some of the specific grooming tips which underpin value.

The following chapters now explain why the Covert Controlled Auction Model should maximise the price obtainable from relevant buyers. In summary the model achieves this through:

1   Finding buyers with most to gain from the acquisition from home and overseas (Chapter 15).

2   Explaining the benefit to buyers of owning the business (Chapter 16).

3   Showing how to negotiate commercially attractive and tax efficient deal structures (Chapter 17).

4   Avoiding the pitfalls of due diligence and legal contracts (Chapter 18).

The next chapter explores how to find buyers.

The Covert Controlled Auction Model

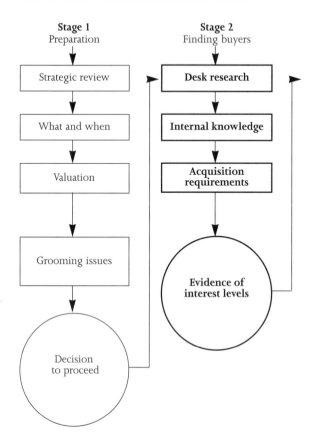

Finding buyers

15

The ability to find the buyer with most to gain from the acquisition is the key to unlocking the maximum consideration from the disposal.

The techniques are similar to those discussed in Chapter 3 but there are important differences when vendors are researching buyers.

Knowledge within the business

Selling is not the opposite of buying. Techniques to alert staff, financial advisors and trade press of your acquisition criteria may be effective but techniques to alert staff are not relevant when selling a business.

Instead, major shareholders and their advisors should meet to discuss possible relevant buyers. These may include previous approaches to the vendor business, larger groups with complementary services, targets with a similar customer base, suppliers to the business, customers to the business and of course direct competitors.

Examples include: training companies who may consider selling to a large business services group; an electronic control systems company may consider selling to a larger engineering group; a film distribution company may be an attractive acquisition for a film production company; or a facilities management business may be an attractive acquisition target for a large construction group eager to shift their activities away from traditionally low margin construction. It is important not to restrict the thinking to merely the vendor's sector but to think broadly of all buyers with most to gain.

Financial institutions

The trend towards institutional buy-outs, ie. venture capitalists acting as financial purchasers should be noted by vendors.

In a recent UK trade sale six out of the eight buyers shortlisted were financial buyers and the top three offers were all made by financial buyers.

Ensure an anonymous one page summary of the vendor business is discussed with a relevant investment director in the key venture capital houses.

In this scenario the agenda for the main shareholder can be:

1   exit from the business and allow second tier management to run the business;

2   partially exit from the business, reducing his role and allow a new managing director to be appointed by the venture capitalist; or

3   partially exit to generate some wealth but stay in his present role and use external funds to grow the business faster.

The other agenda for the financial buyer is that they may have an investee company in the vendor's sector keen to grow. On the other hand their investee company may be struggling and the vendor could be seen by them as a solution to their problem.

Management buy-outs (MBOs)

A specific buyer worth mentioning separately at this stage is the MBO team.

How should a vendor deal with an MBO team as a potential acquiror?

The specialist topic of MBOs is outside the scope of this book, however some guidance is offered here from a vendor's perspective.

One way of handling an MBO team is to set a reserve price on the business. Tell the MBO team they have six weeks to deliver an offer at that price subject to due diligence and contract with written evidence of support from a financial institution. They will be given an exclusivity period of six weeks to deliver the offer. Failure to deliver will be transparently clear from the MBO team's perspective and therefore they cannot complain about the Group Board subsequently choosing another route for exit.

On the other hand if the vendor runs a competitive auction (in the public sector it is compulsory) involving the MBO team there are several risks to be aware of. Firstly, external acquirors may be surprised by the pessimism voiced by senior members of the vendor management team regarding the future prospects of the business! Secondly, some acquirors will not bid for businesses whilst an MBO is being pursued due to the danger of senior managers leaving if their MBO fails. Finally, it is difficult for the vendor to ensure that all buyers have access to the same level of information i.e. the MBO team has a knowledge of the business which buyers may never attain.

Research buyers worldwide

Quality desk research for worldwide buyers starts with names and sectors produced by the brainstorming session described earlier under 'Knowledge within the business'.

These ideas set out the obvious sectors and segments from which buyers are likely to emerge and coupled with the advisor's knowledge of the sector form the basis of a worldwide search. It is surprising the attraction of a small unquoted vendor to a large overseas player who needs a foothold in the UK.

The desk research tools described in Chapter 3 are relevant in finding buyers:

UK

- Kompass
- Kellys
- Key British Enterprises
- Macmillans
- Hambro's

USA

- Moodys directories
- Hoovers
- Standard & Poors directories

Europe

- Hoppenstedt – Germany, Switzerland, Austria
- Kompass – most countries
- Dun-Bradstreet – most countries
- Creditreform – Germany, France

Far East

- Graham and Trotman directories

- Kompass

As mentioned earlier the task is to track down as many potential buyers from as many relevant sectors as possible. Vendors should not confine themselves to searching in their own sector if they wish to be sure they have all relevant buyers in the ring.

Another source of names is the worldwide purchasers of businesses similar to the vendor's business. There are many acquisition databases, as described in Chapter 4, which will detail most deals done worldwide in a sector.

Establish acquisition criteria

Researching, comprehensively, the potential buyers of a business using the above techniques is a necessary important step but it is theory. The next step is to select a list of up to 20 names and establish their acquisition criteria. Acquisitive groups can turn off the tap on acquisitions overnight. Therefore even if vendors are aware of an acquisitive group's criteria from six months ago, it may be out of date.

Establish the acquiring group's current strategy and area of focus. Are they concentrating on the Far East, Europe or specifically the UK? Are they considering diversification or are they sticking to their core area of activity?

At the end of this exercise vendors should have considerable comfort that there is potential interest from buyers in their type of business. The buyers will not know at this stage that the vendor's business is for sale.

A decision can now be made within the vendor's camp whether to proceed to the next stage – buyer contact.

The Covert Controlled Auction Model

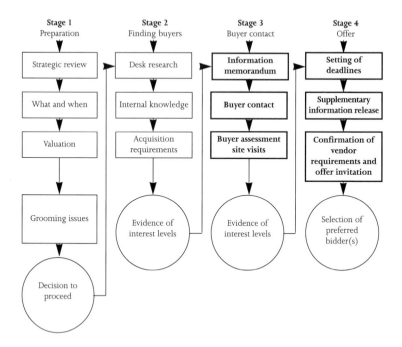

Buyer contact and information release

16

This is the stage of the Covert Controlled Auction Model when the vendor discovers the real interest level of potential acquirors. However before contact is made an Information Memorandum needs to be produced.

Information memorandum

The objective of a well written information memorandum is to illustrate the quality and strengths of a business. It must cover the ground in terms of detail, but verbosity will turn off busy senior executives of potential acquirors.

An executive summary is essential, highlighting the salient points: financials, achievements, activities, people and strategy for growth.

The main chapter headings will include:

1 Executive summary

2 History and background

3 Activities and premises

4 Customers and suppliers

5 Quality achievements

6   Market position

7   Shareholding base

8   Management and staff

9   Financial performance

10 Strategy for growth

Appendices may include the latest statutory accounts, product brochures and perhaps a plan of the site.

The tone should be upbeat and ideally establish in the buyer's mind, from the outset, why the vendor business is a strong strategic fit.

A point of detail on the financials is that forecasts should be excluded except for the current year. Historical results should clearly show one off costs and owner benefits. Ensure the evidence exists to support these add backs.

Buyer contact

Contact should be made at the acquiror's Group Board level to confirm the investment opportunity. An anonymous one page summary is often helpful to clarify telephone conversations. Obtain a signed confidentiality letter before releasing the Information Memorandum.

Care is required when dealing with UK subsidiary management of overseas parent companies. The authority to complete acquisitions will often rest with the overseas board. Therefore be careful not to release confidential information to middle managers with no authority to transact acquisitions.

Often at this stage in the process the manner in which buyers respond to the opportunity illustrates their approach to acquisitions. Many acquisitive groups will appear sharp, will sign off the confidentiality letter and will be keen to both read and respond to the Information Memorandum.

On the other hand, sadly, some acquisitive groups let themselves down even at this early stage. One page summaries take weeks to review, confidentiality letters are changed over and over again as their lawyers redraft the original version. Unfortunately this approach is often carried through to a ponderous style of investigation and a lack of focus at the offer stage.

As a vendor, you need to stage manage all of the responses to the initial contact keeping all parties at the same stage and on a level playing field.

Initial meetings and site visits

The initial meeting with a buyer is an opportunity to both explain the quality of the vendor business and to understand how it may fit with the acquiror's group.

Chapters 5 and 6 described how an acquiror gathers information on the business and its management, including site visits.

The key issue for the vendor from these meetings is how much information should be released. This will depend on how many rounds of bidding are envisaged.

Commercially sensitive information can be held back and released at the due diligence phase if it merely confirms an assumption.

Stage manage site visits, ideally meeting off site initially at a nearby hotel. A formal site visit to the premises can then be hosted by the vendor if the acquiror seems genuinely keen and appears to offer a strong strategic fit.

Vendors should understand the post acquisition strategy of the acquiror and what the specific acquiror will bring to the vendor. This latter point may be more relevant to the private company owner who is transferring to the acquiror to develop the business, than it is to a Group Board member selling a non-core subsidiary.

Query the acquiror's track record on previous acquisitions. How do they approach due diligence? What do they seek in terms of warranties and indemnities?

After these initial meetings the vendor can then decide in an informed way whether there is real interest in the business. Assuming there are at least two or more parties keen to move ahead then the formal procedure of receiving offers can get underway.

Offer stage

It is helpful at this stage for acquirors to be formally informed of the procedure for submitting an offer. In large disposal exercises from the private sector and in disposals from the public sector it is normal to set out the timetable to formal offers within the Information Memorandum.

However in smaller unquoted disposals (less than £25m) it may be more effective to clarify the level of interest from acquirors before setting aggressive timetables which are in danger of being ignored or turning away potential purchasers.

This is also the opportunity to issue supplementary packs of information to acquirors to ensure they have sufficient information on which to bid.

A vendor's requirements should be made clear to all acquirors i.e.:

1   Price for the entire share capital.

2   If an earn-out has been discussed, then clear examples of the
    formula to be used should be illustrated to demonstrate potential
    consideration.

3 The acquiror's treatment of intercompany debt.

4 The acquiror's view of net assets at completion.

5 Any conditions attaching to the bid should be clarified.

6 Any regulatory constraints should be clarified.

7 The need for letters of support from funding sources.

8 The acquiror's post acquisition strategy.

9 The acquiror's due diligence required.

10 The acquiror's timetable to completion.

The vendors can now consider, with the help of their advisors, in an informed way the best way forward.

Tactics at this stage depend heavily on the number, quality, and complexity of the offers.

However, it is recommended that several clarification meetings are set up with the shortlisted parties to confirm detailed aspects of their offers.

This may lead to further information being released to all parties and a request to all parties after these meetings to confirm their best offer.

This should allow the vendor to choose a preferred bidder to enter into final negotiations.

The Covert Controlled Auction Model

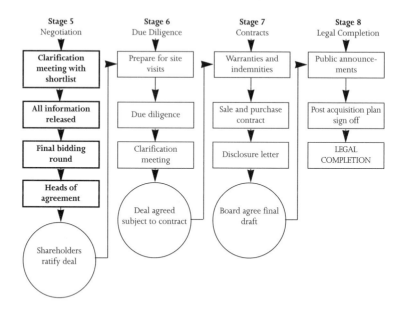

Negotiating attractive deal structures and tax efficiency

17

Many of the relevant techniques for structuring unquoted acquisitions were discussed in Chapter 9. However we examine below some tips for vendors when entering this important stage in the process and in the second half of the chapter we discuss the Heads of Agreement meeting from a vendor's perspective.

Assets or shares

As mentioned earlier there are only two ways of selling a business: assets or shares.

From a vendor's perspective:

Advantage – selling assets

- To crystallise a capital gain in a group of companies to make use of a capital loss.

Disadvantages – selling assets

- Risk of the double tax trap – the capital gain on the disposal of the assets is taxed within the business and if the surplus cash is then distributed to shareholders then each shareholder is taxed on receipt of the dividend.

- Separate negotiation of apportionment of consideration required.

- The history of the business remains with the corporate entity. Therefore instead of the vendor selling up without any connections with the past (with the exception of warranties and indemnities), the vendor is left with a corporate entity with a trading history and no assets except a pile of cash.

- The administration of winding up the company.

Advantages – selling shares

- Taxed once on disposal of shares.

- Transfer the history of the company to the buyer.

- Obtain value for any trading tax losses.

- Avoid balancing charges.

Disadvantage – selling shares

- Strong warranties and indemnities will be expected by buyers.

Types of consideration

It may sound strange to say that a cash consideration is tax inefficient but when considering tax planning for a vendor the statement is true if commercially naive.

Over the years there have been many tax schemes aimed at deferring or avoiding tax on the sale of a company. Many of these tax loop holes have been closed – for example, the exporting of shares into an overseas trust. However, the following tips should assist vendors in minimising their tax liabilities at completion.

Ultimately a vendor can emigrate and avoid paying tax unless cash receipts from the sale are remitted to the UK. However as a vendor there is merit in carefully considering the quality of life option of living in the

UK and paying tax compared with living overseas with more disposable wealth.

Cash received at completion for the sale of a vendor's shares will crystallise a capital gain and therefore be taxed.

The receipt of **paper** – shares, loanstock, preference shares or debentures – as consideration for a vendor's shares will not crystallise a capital gain until the 'paper' received is redeemed. This is a simplification but if the deal is carefully structured it should hold true.

There are specific rules governing earn-outs regarding cash and paper which we will deal with later.

The commercial issues for a vendor accepting 'paper' instead of cash surround the issue of security and value.

The receipt of **shares** in a large listed group may deliver a material gain for the vendor. On the other hand, if the vendor had access to a large tranche of cash, would one invest in a single company's shares?

The risk of taking any proportion of the consideration in the form of shares must be a personal judgement call. Of course, some small listed acquirors may attempt to cajole vendors into believing the growth of their share price is inevitable.

Redeemable preference shares offered by the acquiror may offer a safer value with the added benefit of a fixed dividend stream. However, if the acquiring group were to go into receivership, there would almost certainly be no redemption and there is no corresponding upside of a potential capital gain from preference shares.

Bank guaranteed loanstock offers the security of cash with the ability to defer tax until the loanstock is redeemed. It is reasonable for vendors to expect some form of interest to be paid on the loanstock prior to redemption. Acquirors will often put a long-stop date on the redemption of these instruments to maintain control of medium-term funding needs.

Another technique worth considering is the **pre-completion dividend**. This was illustrated in Chapter 9. It should be noted that the constraint on this technique is not necessarily the ability to fund the dividend out of cash in the vendor balance sheet but rather the level of distributable reserves in the balance sheet. From a negotiation point of view it is worth establishing whether new medium-term finance will be put in place by the acquiror post completion as a pre-completion dividend of any material nature will have temporarily reduced the vendor's working capital.

Other forms of consideration are likely to fall into the category of 'sweeteners' rather than material tranches of consideration for the vendor's shares e.g. one-off pension contributions, private assets being transferred, service agreements and consultancy arrangements.

An interesting angle worth investigating with the acquiror, as mentioned earlier, is restrictive covenants. If the acquiror feels strongly that a restrictive covenant is appropriate, then a vendor should request a separate payment for this concession. If properly structured this payment should be tax allowable for the acquiror.

Earn-out deals

This is the term to describe the disposal of the entire share capital of the company for consideration at completion plus the potential to earn another tranche of consideration based on the future performance of the vendor business.

Earn-outs have been described in Chapter 10; however there are many dangers for vendors in these types of deal structures.

	Problem areas	Solution
1	The buyer goes into receivership prior to payment of earn-out.	The earn-out payments should be bank guaranteed, payable on achievement of performance or if earlier the buyer's receivership.
2	The buyer is acquired during the earn-out period.	Contract should honour earn-out arrangement or the full earn-out is payable on take-over.
3	The vendor business is ring-fenced through the earn-out period.	Identifiable marketing, development, research costs of a material nature with potentially long-term benefits can be accounted for outside of the earn-out formula e.g. costs and income.
4	The vendor may have one bad year within the earn-out.	The use of averages in the formula can minimise the impact.
5	Accounting policies of buyer harsher than vendor.	Vendor's accounting policies are used for earn-out purposes.
6	Acquiror's auditors may take a conservative line on recognising profits within the vendor business.	Joint auditors appointed during earn-out.
7	Service contract expires prior to reviewing final earn-out year.	Ensure service contracts run until at least 6 months after the last earn-out year.

157

8	If cash is offered for the earn-out consideration up to a maximum, a capital gain will crystallise at completion related to all consideration not just the initial tranche.	The acceptable solution is to structure the earn-out consideration in the form of paper, preferably bank guaranteed loan notes. If well structured the gain on the deferred element should not crystallise until the 'paper' is redeemed.
9	Finally the acquiror may attempt to cross charge a range of expenses post completion to suppress profits.	The rules of engagement and definition of earn-out profit should be articulated in the sale and purchase contract to avoid confusion.

Another spin on the earn-out structure offered to vendors is the opportunity to run the acquiror's division (healthy or ill?) as well as the vendor business post completion. The vendor is put on an earn-out structure running both businesses. Before accepting this structure vendors will need to conduct rigorous due diligence on the buyer's division in question but it is possible to structure an earn-out in such circumstances.

The above gives some clues to vendors on the pitfalls to watch for in negotiating deals. It is worth mentioning, before leaving the subject of negotiation, the importance of the Heads of Agreement meeting from the vendor's perspective.

Heads of agreement meeting

The vendor will have selected a preferred bidder, keeping at least one other party on stand-by in the event of negotiations breaking down with the preferred party.

Remember, from a vendor's perspective the purpose of this meeting is to extract the best possible offer from the acquiror prior to due diligence and contract.

Both sides to the deal should come to this meeting with all mandates in place from their respective Boards and a willingness to shake hands on a deal or agree there is no deal to be done.

Negotiation styles are a personal judgement call and outside the scope of this book. Experience shows that professional one-upmanship, bluffing and snide comments are unhelpful tactics in this meeting.

A suggested agenda is discussed in Chapter 10 but vendors must ensure the specific issues that require clarification are dealt with at the beginning of the meeting.

Specifically in earn-out deals, time should be spent discussing the up front sum. Remember the business is being sold at completion and therefore the consideration paid at completion must reflect the loss of control. Only when all issues have been exhausted regarding this element should the deferred element be reviewed.

The meeting is also an opportunity to clarify again the acquiror's post acquisition strategy. Has the acquiror grasped the full potential of owning the vendor business?

Another problem area for these meetings is recent good or bad news concerning either party but mainly the vendor. How do you handle a new sales order materially affecting value? How do you handle the resignation of a key member of staff?

No matter how much planning has gone into the Heads of Agreement meeting there are often surprises, good or bad, to be dealt with.

This is why it is important to clarify the other side's position before embarking on your strategy for the meeting.

The meeting is also an important forum to agree the extent of due diligence to be conducted by the acquiror. It would seem only fair to warn the acquiror that due diligence is not an opportunity to draft the 'fiddler's charter', i.e. there is a danger that the deal will terminate if the acquiror attempts to re-negotiate the terms downwards after due diligence.

The important point to note, in summary, is that if agreement is reached, it is imperative that it is articulated in sufficient detail to cover all the issues, be deliverable from a tax and legal standpoint and show (using worked examples) the meaning of the deal structure. (This is very important for briefing lawyers who find numbers difficult!).

Note: in the UK, Heads of Agreements are not normally legally binding but are an agreement to agree.

Finally, we review in the next and final chapter of the book the due diligence and legal stage from a vendor's perspective.

The Covert Controlled Auction Model

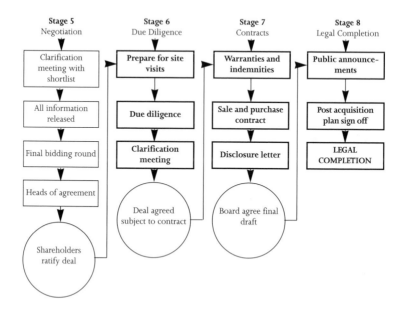

Due diligence
and contracts

18

Due diligence

In the acquisition of an unquoted company a vendor has to accept that due diligence is a necessary evil in closing a deal.

Despite claims to the contrary, it is possible to stage manage an efficient due diligence process without a vendor's staff knowing that the business is for sale.

Cover stories need to be put in place. Finance raising, grant assessment, insurance advice or pensions advice are all helpful excuses as well as the obvious auditor disguise.

Acquirors should require no more than two weeks on site and preferably one.

Vendors should prepare for due diligence. Examine the checklist in Appendix III for the likely items that will be reviewed.

Senior managers may need to be brought into the disclosure net if they are to be interviewed by the acquisition team.

If confidentiality does start to breakdown, the vendor and acquiror may have to issue some form of words along the lines that advanced discussions have been entered into which may lead to an offer for the company being made. For a listed company there are stock exchange implications if information starts to leak.

If the vendor is nervous of releasing specific commercially sensitive information, e.g. complicated price structures with key customers, then a negotiation tactic may be to request similar information from the acquiror.

Especially when an earn-out is envisaged, the vendor should take this opportunity to do some detailed due diligence on the buyer.

Previous deals done by the acquiror are usually good reference points for vendors to seek comfort on the post acquisition behaviour of buyers.

Finally, it is important for vendors to set a deadline regarding due diligence. Acquirors will continue to investigate the target over many months given the chance. The acquiror should clarify that all due diligence matters have been dealt with and that the timetable to completion is still on schedule.

Sale and purchase contracts – non-lawyer tips

It is common for the buyer to prepare the legal documentation.

This allows the vendors to establish control over the final phase of the deal, detailing precisely what is to be said and articulating the acceptable warranties and indemnities to be given.

However, assuming a share sale, it is likely the acquiror will issue the first draft of the sale and purchase contract.

The following list of items should serve to guide the vendor over the final hurdle before completion:

1   Ensure your lawyer minimises the extent and duration of
    warranties and indemnities.

2 If net assets are to be audited as part of the deal, attempt to agree a cut-off date one month prior to completion and ensure the completion statement is produced for completion. This avoids the vendor arguing over the level of net assets at completion, some months after completion, when the vendor may not be managing the business. Alternatively the acquiror may retain some of the consideration – 'a retention' – to be allocated later once net assets are completed.

3 Warranty claims must be capped at disposal proceeds and preferably less.

4 Watch for over keen lawyers' point scoring and move in to close down points of little commercial substance.

5 Remember to operate on a 'package' basis when negotiating. Small concessions from the vendor's perspective may be valued highly by acquirors. Collect a range of concessions to be given to get the big concession that minimises your risk.

6 Acquirors will attempt to secure main points of principle throughout the agreement. Recognise the important issues from their perspective without conceding all the warranties the acquiror may request. For example, an acquiror may request that all information supplied to him in the course of the acquisition should be warranted. Vendors should reject this in favour of, perhaps, warranting key facts upon which the acquiror is relying.

Several drafting meetings will be required between the parties before a final sale and purchase contract is produced.

In addition vendors should carefully consider the **Disclosure Letter**.

This sets out all information which, if not disclosed, could be the subject of a claim under the warranties. Depending on the specific warranties given, it can cover any aspect of the business. The problems for the vendors in producing comprehensive Disclosure Letters are partly the time constraints under which they are produced and also the ability to remember key facts from the past worth disclosing. Therefore the vendor's lawyer should question the vendor(s) on all key aspects of the business to ensure all relevant facts are disclosed.

Therefore, as a vendor approaches legal completion there should be an advanced version of the sale and purchase contract (usually 80-100 pages) nearing its final version and a formal Disclosure Letter with a bundle of disclosure documents released to the acquiror.

Legal completion and announcements

The formal legal completion meeting can be a low key event or a more upbeat formal signing session between the Principals.

The manner in which the deal is announced and the words within the press release are extremely important. The communication should motivate senior staff on both sides, comfort customers and especially the vendor's customers, inform the City of the details and strategy of the deal (if one of the parties is a listed group) and offer contact numbers for further details if required.

The vendor should also use this final session to confirm the immediate post acquisition action plan of the acquiror.

Appendix I

Commercial due diligence checklist

- ☐ Economic factors affecting the sector
- ☐ Legislative factors affecting the sector
- ☐ Competitive position of the target in the sector
- ☐ Growth statistics of the sector
- ☐ Demographic changes affecting activities of the target
- ☐ Technology risks surrounding target
- ☐ Relevant investment analyst reports on the sector
- ☐ Results from previous years
- ☐ Estimate of target's sales income – next 5 years
- ☐ Estimate of costs – under acquiror's management
- ☐ Effect of acquisition on acquiror's business
- ☐ Net asset value at completion
- ☐ Surplus assets
- ☐ Private owner assets
- ☐ Cost/time of alternatives to acquisition
- ☐ Rarity value of target
- ☐ Acquiror's accounting policies – effect on vendor profits
- ☐ Post acquisition management structure
- ☐ Cost of services to be provided by acquiror
- ☐ One-off costs reducing historical profits
- ☐ One-off credits enhancing vendor profits

Commercial due diligence checklist

- ☐ Owner benefit costs quantified
- ☐ Order book – asset or liability
- ☐ Pricing opportunities
- ☐ Capital expenditure required
- ☐ Cost of refurbishments
- ☐ Patent related costs
- ☐ Litigation provisions
- ☐ Balance sheet – adequacy of provisions, stock, debtors
- ☐ Environmental concerns
- ☐ Contingent liabilities
- ☐ Property valuations
- ☐ Production capacity and efficiencies
- ☐ Research and development – on-going costs
- ☐ Price Earnings Ratio (PER) of previous deals done
- ☐ PER of quoted company equivalent to target

Appendix II

Post acquisition planning checklist

(A financial checklist covering post acquisition planning is dealt with under Appendix I Commercial due diligence)

Strategy

☐ What is the key competitive advantage of the business? Why are you buying it?

☐ Is it for products, distribution, earnings, expansion into new markets?

☐ Can that competitive advantage be sustained after any acquisition?

☐ Do you fully understand the nature of the business you are buying?

☐ How has the strategy been developed – deliberately or by chance?

☐ How is the strategy currently reviewed?

☐ How will the strategy impact on the acquiror's business?

Culture and management style

☐ Autocratic – participative – paternalistic?

☐ Personality or skills based – dominant founder or quality management team?

☐ Performance culture – business performance, people appraisals, assessment?

☐ Strong financial and cost control culture?

☐ Quality culture?

☐ Customer focused culture?

☐ Marketing or sales driven culture?

Post acquisition planning checklist

☐ Production or R&D culture?

☐ Nature of management and staff relationships? – Union(s) involvement?

☐ Quality second layer of management?

☐ Employee involvement – training, suggestion schemes, recognition?

☐ Investors in People accreditation?

Customer and service quality

☐ Clear policy or objectives on quality ISO 9000?

☐ Key customer service measures plus any results, trends etc?

☐ Specific programmes and initiatives to promote quality and service – past and present?

☐ Service standards linked to recruitment and training?

☐ Service training for staff?

☐ Communications processes for quality and service?

People

☐ What are the backgrounds and experience of the owners and management?

☐ What are the backgrounds of key staff and staff in general?

☐ Who are the critical staff?

☐ Family relationships present?

☐ What are the relative strengths and weaknesses of the people involved?

Post acquisition planning checklist

☐ Are there any critical retirements coming up?

☐ Do people understand their roles and how they contribute towards business performance?

☐ Do people know what are the expected standards of performance?

☐ Are staff loyal to the business? What staff turnover has the business experienced?

☐ What encourages staff retention? – pay, work environment, owners behaviour, convenience?

☐ What investment has been made in the skills of staff and management in general?

☐ Does the business suffer in any area as a result of skill shortages?

☐ What is the general length of service profile of staff?

☐ Are pay and benefits competitive – business markets and general labour market?

Systems

☐ What is the general status and credibility of the business's management information systems?

☐ To what extent do the systems seem reactive or proactive to business development?

☐ What is the quality of the financial management control systems?

☐ Customer databases?

☐ What is computerised and what is manual?

☐ What are the current costs of maintaining the systems?

Post acquisition planning checklist

☐ Are there any plans to update these systems?

☐ What are staff views on these systems?

☐ Are there any systems for measuring or managing staff performance?

Structure

☐ What is the formal management structure of the business?

☐ To what extent does the formal structure reflect the reality of how the business is run?

☐ Are there any issues surrounding the existing structure – conflicts between sales and production?

☐ Review job titles and question beyond them.

☐ Do people have appropriate levels of authority?

☐ Is the structure too complex?

☐ Is the structure focused around the customer or the organisation?

☐ How would the structure fit into any new owner's structure?

Financial

(See Appendix I – Commercial due diligence checklist)

Appendix III

Due diligence checklist

Plan of a detailed long-form due diligence or investigation report

1 Executive summary

2 History and description of business

History & development

☐ Corporate name and address of parent company; country and date of incorporation; subsequent name changes.

☐ Brief history and significant events since incorporation; significant changes in controlling ownership. Brief details on growth in turnover, profits, assets and employees.

Group organisation

☐ Names and addresses of companies and divisions in the group; extent of holdings in subsidiary undertakings; countries and dates of incorporation; dates of acquisition; trading activities; auditors. Key locations and premises.

Statistical information

☐ For the group and each main activity: total personnel employed; total net tangible assets; total earnings before tax for latest year; return on net tangible assets. Relative size in local markets and internationally, with brief details of major competitors.

Due diligence checklist (continued)

☐ Statistics for the relevant period of the industry/industries as a whole, including the market background, and appropriate price indices to measure the effect of inflation.

Capital structure

☐ Particulars of the authorised and issued share capital of parent company, divided by classes of shares.

☐ Voting and other powers of the various classes of shares; recent share issues; major shareholdings; share options.

☐ Share performance (if quoted); total market capitalisation; investment ratings.

Corporate objectives

☐ Brief summary of corporate objectives and philosophy; present and desired corporate perceptions.

3 Management and employees

Management structure

☐ Charts of functional and line management responsibilities. Key head office functions; method of control.

☐ Frequency of meetings of directors and other management committees. Details of other committees' duties and membership.

Directors and senior or key management

☐ Names and responsibilities; positions held; ages; remuneration; length of service; qualifications; location; nationality; shareholdings and other directorships; service agreements; pension rights; life insurance cover; cars; other fringe benefits.

Due diligence checklist (continued)

☐ Competence of management, including assessment of the strengths and weaknesses of management, identifying any gaps; management succession; experience; quality of leadership; unutilised potential.

☐ Management development; training projects; recruitment procedure; remuneration review procedure; bonus incentive schemes.

☐ Management philosophy and culture, approach to problem solving and decision making.

☐ Corporate governance issues, non-executive directors, audit committee.

Employees

☐ Analyses by location and function; dependence upon skilled labour; sources; rates paid by the group and by its competitors. Details of personnel department's, effectiveness and responsibilities.

Methods of remunerating labour

☐ Method and level of pay, including incentive schemes; job description; union involvement; redundancy payments (history and detail of any schemes); pension schemes; health care; post-retirement benefits; life insurance cover; housing; cars; personal loan scheme; staff welfare; holiday entitlements.

Staff and labour relations

☐ Working conditions; accident frequency; staff turnover; key personnel losses; strike record; productivity (compare with competitors); union involvement; recruitment and training schemes.

Due diligence checklist (continued)

☐ Employee morale; team spirit; promotion of initiative and self reliance; encouragement of ingenuity and responsibility. Management communication with unions/workforce.

4 Accounting records and management information

Financial accounting records

☐ Nature of records and equipment used to maintain them; whether kept up to date; general reliability and efficiency; manual of accounting instructions; account codes; management letters from the auditors.

☐ Arrangements for management accounting information; frequency; speed of preparation; accuracy; basis of preparation (especially concerning stock valuation and provisions against assets); staffing; information produced; reconciliation with financial accounts; year-end adjustments.

Costing systems

☐ Type of costing systems employed; integration with financial accounts; adequacy and reliability.

Information technology

☐ IT strategy; details of facilities; management of IT; attitude to IT; intangible value of IT.

Budgetary control

☐ Soundness and appropriateness of system; effectiveness of action taken on variances; control techniques; frequency of updating; accuracy and reliability of past budgets.

Due diligence checklist (continued)

Foreign exchange management

☐ Exposure to fluctuations, reporting of exposure/risk; hedging policies.

Forecasting

☐ History; system; reliability; whether realistic; profits; net assets; cash flow.

☐ Corporate planning; strategic and annual reviews; planning cycle; responsibilities; strategic options.

Information supplied to management

☐ Summary of reporting guidelines; usefulness; clarity; brevity and timeliness.

☐ Effectiveness of management communication; policy manuals; operating instructions; liaison committees; office circulars; house journals; staff meetings.

☐ Information on legal matters; in-house expertise; name of solicitors; history of litigation; recent disputes; recent legal representation letters.

5 Marketing

Main product lines

☐ Description and history of main product lines; quality; unique factors; trade names; patents; trade marks and registered designs.

☐ Three year record of product sales performance in quantity and value; highlight seasonal patterns and shifts in patterns; stock requirements; order position; sales backlog.

Due diligence checklist (continued)

Main markets, customers and distribution methods

☐ Size of market; nature of market (growing/mature); market share; home and export; main customers; method of distribution; own transport and storage.

☐ Sales incentives; control over distribution channels and outlets; licensing; joint ventures.

Terms of trade

☐ Pricing policy; credit agreements; right of return; special discounts; intra-group sales; export arrangements and restrictions; government business; long-term contracts.

☐ Delivery record; penalty clauses; after sales service; trade associations; monopolies and restrictive practices legislation; EU legislation.

Competitors and competitive products

☐ Competitors' products and potential; estimated share of market; marketing policy; recent successes and failures and reasons therefore; special features of competition.

Promotion

☐ Advertising; sponsorship; exhibitions; expenditure as a percentage of turnover compared with major competitors.

Market analysis

☐ Research of publications and reports to determine past and likely future trends based on annual and projected economics of the industry or trade; three to five year forecast of growth or contraction in the relevant markets.

Due diligence checklist (continued)

☐ Estimate of industry's ability to supply present and expected demand; effect and probability of change in government policy.

☐ Review of internal factors affecting current sales; sales volumes and pricing policies; credit terms; productive capacity; planning for new products; new product lines to meet technological advances; sales management organisation; advertising and promotion campaigns; salesmen's incentive schemes; customer contacts; reliability of services.

☐ Analysis of present and potential domestic and export customers to highlight new areas for marketing expansion; special discount and credit terms for incentive purposes; loss leaders retained in development of new markets; where significant, analyse distribution costs to determine most profitable areas and products; consider customers; reactions to products.

☐ Comparison of sales and cost projections with actual over past three years; sales, cancellations and returns; sales and expenses analysed by salesman; customer services costs, shifts in product mix and effect on profit margins; order processing costs; customer complaints and lost customers; new accounts opened.

☐ Three to five year projections of company's sales expectations and estimate of market share; underlying commercial assumptions; order-book position.

☐ New product development; product life cycles; present plans for new products.

Due diligence checklist (continued)

6 Production, purchasing and research and development

Production strategy

☐ Own manufacture; subcontracting, 'just in time'; to order or for stock.

Existing production facilities and current usage

☐ Location, size and condition of factories and major plant installations; development areas; description of assembly lines; production techniques; power sources; local infrastructure.

☐ Description of production process and key elements; current production capacity usage; unused capacity; organisation and division of manufacturing responsibility; labour force utilisation; shift and overtime working; production planning; material handling techniques; control of work-in-progress; use of subcontractors; licensing arrangements; basis of manufacturing planning.

☐ Assessment of senior production officials; technical competence; managerial abilities and leadership potential.

Manufacturing efficiency

☐ Standard cost variance analysis; comments on fluctuations and trends of material and labour usage; labour efficiency; capacity utilisation; break-even levels; spoilage and product rejections; defective production; idle time; absenteeism; delays in delivery times.

Due diligence checklist (continued)

☐ Critical lead times of machines, tooling etc; routing schedules; machine times; materials handling; efficiency of production and layout.

☐ Quality control arrangements; incidence of waste, scrap; rejects and returns; customer satisfaction.

☐ Review of detailed manufacturing overhead costs and comparisons with earlier years; comparison of production costs with industry-wide production cost data where available.

Future requirements

☐ Assessment of likely capital investment requirements; comment on assumptions underlying forecast; new products planned.

Purchasing organisation

☐ Description and status of purchasing function; purchasing department personnel; departmental or divisional organisation.

☐ Co-ordination with production, research and development and quality control divisions; requisitioning routines; purchasing, re-ordering and approval procedures.

Purchasing policy

☐ Sources and terms of supply of raw materials; alternative sources of supply; monopoly suppliers; past needs of raw materials and bought-in components; warehousing facilities; stock requirements; purchase contracts.

☐ Estimate of future requirements; underlying assumptions; changes due to technological developments; effects of government policies on imports.

Due diligence checklist (continued)

Research and development strategy and facilities

☐ Strategy; pure or applied research; in-house or third parties; comparison with competitors.

☐ Location and layout of facilities; description of personnel; qualifications; experience; technical talents; managerial competence and leadership potential.

☐ Recent, current and planned projects.

☐ Details of trade marks, patents and other such rights.

Product planning

☐ Run-down and self-developed products nearing end of economic life; production planning for new products being introduced; further projects under development; new techniques now in use; own product and techniques sold elsewhere under licence; important patents owned.

Environmental matters

☐ Impact of current and future environmental legislation on sources of raw materials, production facilities and general business activities; use and ultimate disposal of finished products; existing and potential costs, liabilities and contingent liabilities.

7 Trading results

Accounting policies

☐ Explain and comment on significant accounting policies; changes in policies during years under review.

Due diligence checklist (continued)

Summary of results

☐ Turnover; gross profit; overheads; net profit; percentages; earnings per share; return on capital employed; variations from budget.

Sales and gross profits of main activities

☐ Analysis of turnover and gross profits over main companies, divisions and products; comment on significant fluctuations.

Analysis of overhead expenses

☐ Main classes of overheads; comment on significant fluctuations.

Adjusted profits before tax (where appropriate)

☐ Computation of adjusted profits; reason for adjustments.

Explanations and comments on trends disclosed

☐ Ratio analysis; trend of gross profit to turnover; exceptional profits or losses; whether profits have kept pace with inflation; currency realignments.

8 Assets and liabilities

Summary of consolidated balance sheet

☐ Statement of net assets; statements of share capital and reserves.

Comments on main assets and liabilities

Fixed assets

☐ Deal separately with property, plant and machinery, vehicles, fixtures and fittings; title; recent acquisitions or disposals; basis of valuation; effects of inflation; cost of replacement; rates of depreciation; in-house manufacture of capital equipment.

Due Diligence Checklist (continued)

☐ Alternative valuation (if available); accounting policy for capitalising interest and expenditure on repairs and renewals; extent to which own labour used for capital work; plant register. Fixed assets held under finance leases.

Intangible assets

☐ Goodwill; patents, copyrights; brands; capitalised research and development; valuation; amortisation policy.

Associated undertakings

☐ Names; activities; shareholding; loans to; cost and underlying net tangible asset value; justification for carrying value.

☐ Terms of trade with associated undertakings.

Investments

☐ Basis of valuation of quoted and unquoted investments; directors' valuation of unquoted investments; results of investment policy; income received.

Stock and work-in-progress

☐ Location; method of valuation; definition of cost and market value; treatment of overheads; provision for slow-moving stock and obsolescence; inter-company profits; variances; cut-off procedures; profits on long-term contracts; provision for loss-making contracts; government costed contracts not settled; physical counts; inventory records; assessment of inventory control; security; reservation of title; insurance; fire risks; ratio of stock and work-in-progress to turnover; effects of inflation on stock values.

Due diligence checklist (continued)

Debtors

☐ Credit control; discounts allowed; bad debts; provision for credit notes; age analysis; factoring of debts; ratio of debtors to turnover; loans to directors/employees; prepayments.

Current liabilities

☐ Credit taken; discounts; reasons for delays in settlement; adequacy of provision for outstanding liabilities; provision against guarantees and warranties given; after-sales service.

☐ Details of pension schemes; actuarial surpluses/deficiencies; unfunded pension commitments; post-retirement benefits.

☐ Litigation pending; claims not settled.

☐ Current and deferred taxation liabilities.

☐ Interest payable; dividends proposed.

Borrowings

☐ Details of all borrowings (including bank overdrafts, loans, finance leases). Terms of borrowings (security, repayment schedule, rate of interest, covenants).

Shareholders' funds

☐ Share capital; share option schemes; distributable/non-distributable reserves.

☐ Transfers of assets at other than market value.

Cash flows

☐ Cash flow statements for the last three years with appropriate comments.

Due diligence checklist (continued)

Insurance cover

☐ Description of key policies and risks covered (plant, property, employer's liability and loss of profits); recent claims and losses; adequacy of cover.

9 Prospects

Budgeted results for current year

☐ Sales; gross profits; overheads; profits before tax; analysis by division or product, as appropriate; tax charge.

☐ Results to date from management accounts; comment on these results and the reliability of previous management accounts.

☐ Confirmation that accounting policies are consistent with last accounts.

Forecast results for subsequent periods

☐ Sales; gross profits; overheads; profits before tax; analysis by division or product, as appropriate; whether profits are likely to keep pace with inflation; tax charge; comments.

☐ Confirmation that accounting policies are consistent with last accounts.

Assumptions underlying budgets/forecasts

☐ Main assumptions concerning sales, marketing, purchasing, production, research and development; areas of vulnerability; effect on forecasts of changes in key assumptions (where possible); comments.

Due diligence checklist (continued)

Comments on reliability of budgets/forecasts

☐ Realistic or targets; past record of success in forecasting (including cash flows); adequacy of contingency provision; likely out-turn in trading and cash flow terms.

Working capital requirements

☐ Cash flow and balance sheet forecasts for current year and subsequent periods; assumptions; reconcile cash flow forecasts with forecast balance sheets and with forecast profits/losses. Comparison of working capital requirements with financing facilities.

☐ Borrowing powers; restrictions imposed by covenants.

☐ Conversion of unproductive assets into cash.

☐ Conclusions on liquidity position.

Sources of additional finance

☐ Share and loan capital issues; short-term financing facilities; costs of new finance.

☐ Further borrowing powers needed.

☐ Conclusions on financing arrangements.

10 Taxation

Corporate taxation

☐ Extent to which liabilities agreed; outstanding issues; tax administration; tax losses; tax planning; close-company status.

☐ Intra-group transfers at under-value.

Due diligence checklist (continued)

Other taxes

☐ VAT schemes (if applicable); VAT inspections; outstanding issues.

☐ PAYE and national insurance inspections; outstanding issues.

Conclusions and recommendations

Principal conclusions and recommendations

☐ Summary of overall outcome of the work; key areas requiring attention; courses of action open to management to safeguard future position, eliminate problem areas, increase profitability, effect diversification, enhance market position, improve trading conditions, rationalise group activities; other matters of critical importance.

List of other important matters

☐ List of other important matters dealt with earlier in report not necessarily calling for conclusions or recommendations but which should be brought to the reader's attention (cross-referenced to relevant earlier paragraphs).

Appendix IV

Useful sources and addresses

Acquisitions Monthly, Lonsdale House, 7-9 Lonsdale Gardens, Tunbridge Wells, Kent, TN1 1NU. Tel. (01892) 515454.

ASLIB Directory of Information Sources in the UK, edited by Keith Reynard and published by ASLIB, 20 Old Street, London, EC1V 9AP. Tel. (0171) 253 4488.

Benns Media. Published annually in three volumes by Benn Business Information Services Ltd, Sovereign Way, Tonbridge, Kent, TN9 1RQ. Tel. (01732) 362666.

Books and Periodicals On-line, 6th edition 1994, published by Library Alliance, Suite 4c, 264 Lexington Avenue, New York City, NY 10016-4182.

British Library Document Supply Centre, Boston Spa, Wetherby, Yorkshire, LS23 7BQ. Tel. (01937) 546060.

Business Information Focus. Fee-based business information service of the City Business Library. Tel. (0171) 600 1461.

The Business Information Service at the British Library's Science Reference and Information Service, 25 Southampton Buildings, London, WC2A 1AW. Tel. (0171) 412 7454 or (0171) 412 7457 for the fee-based research unit.

CCN Business Information, Abbey House, Abbeyfield Road, Nottingham, NG7 1BR. Tel. (0115) 941 0888.

The CD-ROM Directory. Published annually by TFPL Multimedia, 17-18 Britton Street, London, EC1M 5NQ. Tel. (0171) 251 5522.

CELEX. Produced by the Office for Official Publications of the EU, OP-7 Databases and Electronic Products Unit, 2 Mercier, L-2895 Luxembourg.

Useful sources and addresses (continued)

Central Statistical Office (CSO) see Office for National Statistics.

The City Business Library, 1 Brewers Hall Garden, London, EC2V 5BX. Tel. (0171) 638 8215. A specialist public reference library service provided by the Corporation of the City of London and open to the general public free of charge. See also Business Information Focus.

Companies House. Headquarters: Crown Way, Cardiff, CF4 3UZ, Tel. (01222) 380801. London office: 55-71 City Road, London, EC1Y 1BB, Tel. (0171) 253 9393.

Context Electronic Publishers, Grand Union House, 20 Kentish Town Road, London, NW1 9NR. Tel. (0171) 267 8989.

Croner's A-Z of Business Information Sources. A loose-leaf updating service published by Croner Publications Ltd, London Road, Kingston upon Thames, Surrey, KT2 6SR. Tel. (0181) 547 3333.

Current British Directories. Published by CBD Research Ltd, 15 Wickham Road, Beckenham, Kent, BR3 2JS. Tel. (0181) 650 7745.

Current Serials Received. Published by the British Library Document Supply Centre. (see above)

Datamonitor Ltd, 106 Baker Street, London, W1M 1LA. Tel. (0171) 625 8548.

Data-Star. Knight-Ridder Information Ltd, Haymarket House, 1 Oxendon Street, London, SW1Y 4EE. Tel. (0171) 930 7646. Knight-Ridder owned host with over 300 databases offering worldwide coverage of business news, financial information, market research etc.

Dialog. Knight-Ridder Information Ltd, Haymarket House, 1 Oxendon Street, London, SW1Y 4EE. Tel. (0171) 930 7646. Knight-Ridder owned host with over 400 databases covering business, science, technology, economics etc.

Useful sources and addresses (continued)

Directory of British Associations and Associations in Ireland published by CBD Research Ltd, 15 Wickham Road, Beckenham, Kent, BR3 2JS. Tel. (0181) 650 7745.

Directory of Directors, has appeared annually for over a century, now published in two volumes by Reed Information Services.

Directory of Legislation in Force, published by the Office for Official Publications of the EU.

Disclosure UK, 26-31 Whiskin Street, London, EC1R 0PD. Tel. (0171) 278 7848. Annual reports on the 12,000+ US quoted companies and more limited but still considerable numbers of those of other developed economies. Until recently the focus of their technological development has been on CD-ROM.

Dun & Bradstreet Ltd, Holmers Farm Way, High Wycombe, Buckinghamshire, HP12 4UL. Tel. (01494) 422000.

The Economist Intelligence Unit Ltd, 40 Duke Street, London, W1A 1DW. Tel. (0171) 493 6711.

Engineers Buyers Guide. In its 99th edition (1996). Published by Miller Freeman Information Services, Riverbank House, Angel Lane, Tonbridge, Kent, TN9 1SE. Tel. (01732) 362 666.

Euromonitor Publications, 87-88 Turnmill Street, London, EC1M 5QU. Tel. (0171) 251 8024.

European Commission Information Service, 8 Storeys Gate, London, SW1P 3AT. Tel. (0171) 973 1992.

The Department of Trade and Industry's Export Market Information Centre, Kingsgate House, 66-74 Victoria Street, London. Tel. (0171) 215 5444. Their fee-based service can be contacted on the same number.

Useful sources and addresses (continued)

FAME. Published by Bureau van Dijk Electronic Publishing Ltd, 1 Great Scotland Yard, London, SW1A 2HN. Tel. (0171) 839 2266.

Financial Times Annual Reports Service. Tel. (0181) 770 0770.

Financial Times Business Research Centre, 1 Southwark Bridge, London, SE1 9HL. Tel. (0171) 407 3322.

Findex: worldwide directory of market research reports, studies and surveys published by Euromonitor.

Frost & Sullivan Ltd, Sullivan House, 4 Grosvenor Gardens, London, SW1W 0DH. Tel. (0171) 730 3438.

FT-Extel, Fitzroy House, 13-17 Epworth Street, London, EC2A 4DL. Tel. (0171) 253 3400.

FT Discovery. An end-user business-briefing product from FT Profile (see below). It offers an overview of company intelligence, business news, sector reports, real-time feed etc.

FT Profile, Fitzroy House, 13-17 Epworth Street, London, EC2A 4DL. Tel. (0171) 825 8000. Host with databases giving full-text coverage of international news, financial data, trade press, market research etc.

Full-text Journals On-line, published every six months by Bibliodata, PO Box 61, Needham Heights, Massachusetts 02194.

Gale International Research, North Way, Andover, Hampshire, SP10 5YE. Tel. (01246) 334446.

Guide to Libraries in London, compiled by Valerie McBurney and published by the British Library's Science Reference and Information Service.

Guide to Official Statistics. Published by the Government Statistical Service through HMSO but not updated since 1990.

Useful sources and addresses (continued)

ICC Information Group Ltd, Field House, 72 Oldfield Road, Hampton, Middlesex, TW12 2HQ. Tel. (0181) 783 0755.

ICC Information Services, 16-26 Banner Street, London, EC1Y 8QE. Tel. (0171) 251 4941. ICC Direct provides financial and full-text company accounts, stockbroker reports and market research. Their data is also available via hosts like Dialog and Data-Star and is used by OneSource in their UK company CD-ROMs. ICC also publish Keynote and Business Ratio Reports.

The Infocheck Group, Godmersham Park, Godmersham, Canterbury, Kent, CT4 7DT. Tel. (01227) 81300.

Information Access Company, Watergate House, 13-15 York Buildings, London, WC2N 6JU. Tel. (0171) 930 3933.

Information for Business, Westminster Reference Library, St Martins Street, London, WC2H 7HP. Tel. (0171) 976 1285. The fee-based business information service of Westminster City Council.

Investext. A division of Thomson Financial Services Ltd, 11 New Fetter Lane, London, EC4A 1JN. Tel. (0171) 815 3900.

Jordan & Sons Ltd, 21 St Thomas Street, Bristol, BS1 6JS. Tel. (0117) 9230600.

Kellys. Published annually by Reed Information Services, Windsor Court, East Grinstead House, East Grinstead, West Sussex, RH19 1XB. Tel. (01342) 326972.

Key British Enterprises. Published annually by Dun & Bradstreet Ltd, Holmers Farm Way, High Wycombe, Buckinghamshire, HP12 4UL. Tel. (01494) 422000.

Useful sources and addresses (continued)

Knight-Ridder Information Ltd, Haymarket House, 1 Oxendon Street, London, SW1 4EE. Tel. (0171) 930 5503. Owners of both the Dialog and Data-Star hosts.

Kompass. Published annually by Reed Information Services, Windsor Court, East Grinstead House, East Grinstead, West Sussex, RH19 1XB. Tel. (01342) 326972.

Leatherhead Food Research Association, Randalls Road, Leatherhead, Surrey, KT22 7RY. Tel. (01372) 376761.

London Business School, Sussex Place, Regent's Park, London, NW1 4SA. Tel. (0171) 262 5050 or (0171) 723 3404 for the fee-based Information Service.

Machinery Buyers Guide. Now in its 70th annual edition (1996). Published by Findlay Publications Ltd, Franks Hall, Horton Kirby, Dartford, Kent, DA4 9LL. Tel. (01322) 222 222.

Macmillan's Unquoted Companies. Published annually by Macmillan Direct Ltd, Houndmills, Basingstoke, Hampshire, RG21 6XS. Tel. (01256) 817245.

MAID, The Communications Building, 48 Leicester Square, London, WC2H 7DB. Tel. (0171) 930 6006. Database host with full-text market research, international press and trade journals.

Marketing Surveys Index. A loose-leaf updating service published by Marketing Strategies for Industry (UK) Ltd, Viscount House, River Lane, Saltney, Chester, CH4 8QY. Tel. (01244) 681424.

Market Research: a guide to British Library holdings, compiled by Michael Leydon and published by the British Library's Science Reference and Information Service.

Useful sources and addresses (continued)

Market Research Locator (see Findex).

MarketSearch. International directory of published market research.
Published annually for 20 years by Arlington Management Publications
Ltd, 1 Hay Hill, Berkeley Square, London, W1X 7LF.
Tel. (0171) 495 1940.

McCarthy Information, Manor House, Ash Walk, Warminster, Wiltshire,
BA12 8PY. Tel. (01985) 215151.

Mintel International Group, 18-19 Long Lane, London, EC1A 9HE.
Tel. (0171) 606 6000.

Monopolies & Mergers Commission, 48 Carey Street, London, WC2A
2HX. Tel. (0171) 324 1467.

Office for National Statistics, Government Buildings, Cardiff Road,
Newport, Gwent, NP9 1XG. Tel. (01633) 812812. Enquiries should be
addressed to the London office: Government Offices, Great George
Street, London, SW1P 3AQ. Tel. (0171) 270 6363. Publications include
Annual Abstract of Statistics, Economic Trends, Regional Trends, Family
Expenditure Survey and UK National Accounts. Formed by merger of
Central Statistical Office and Office of Population Censuses and Surveys.

OneSource Information Services Ltd, Dukes Court, Duke Street,
Woking, Surrey, GU21 5BH. Tel. (01483) 241200.

On-line/CD-ROM Business Sourcebook. Published by Headland
Business Information, 1 Henry Smith's Terrace, Headland, Cleveland,
TS24 0PD. Tel. (01429) 231902. Headland Press have recently sold this
title and the 1996/97 edition will be published by Bowker-Saur.

The On-line Manual, edited by Sue Allcock and Linda Whitby, 4th
edition 1996, published by Learned Information Europe Ltd,
Woodside, Hinksey Hill, Oxford, OX1 5BE. Tel. (01865) 730275.

Useful sources and addresses (continued)

PiMS UK Ltd, PiMS House, Midmay Avenue, London, N1 4RS. Tel. (0171) 226 1000. Published quarterly.

PIRA International. Randalls Road, Leatherhead, Surrey, KT22 7RU. Tel. (01372) 376 161.

ProBase. A Knight-Ridder product which offers the full range of databases available from Data-Star in a simple Windows point-and-click environment.

RAPRA Technology Ltd. Shawbury, Shrewsbury, Shropshire, SY4 4NR. Tel. (01939) 250 383.

Retail Business. Published by Corporate Intelligence Group Ltd, 51 Doughty Street, London, WC1N 2LS. Tel. (0171) 696 9006.

Reuters Ltd, 85 Fleet Street, London, EC4P 4AJ. Tel. (0171) 250 1122. Full-text articles and long abstracts from c.2,200 sources dating back to 1980. This has consistently been the most popular database in the UK library/research market. Available on the Knight-Ridder hosts, MAID and via a gateway on FT Profile.

Taylor Nelson AGB, 14-17 St John's Square, London, EC1M 4HE. Tel. (0171) 608 0072.

Thomson Financial Services Ltd, 11 New Fetter Lane, London, EC4A 1NN. Tel. (0171) 815 3800.

Who's Who in Industry. Published by Fulcrum Publishing, 254 Goswell Road, London, EC1V 7EB. Tel. (0171) 253 0353.

Who's Who in the City. Published by Macmillan Press, 4 Little Essex Street, London, WC2R 3LF. Tel. (0171) 836 6633.

Willings Press Guide, has appeared annually for over 120 years, now in two volumes, by Reed Business Information Services (see Kompass and Kellys).